Guided Meditations for Anxiety

Beginner Meditation to Cure Anxiety,
Panic Attacks and Depression

Table of Contents

Introduction

Welcome to, "Guided Meditations for Anxiety: Beginner Meditation to Cure Anxiety, Panic Attacks and Depression". Thank you for purchasing this volume. It is great to see that you have chosen this book among others in this category.

In this book, you will find a detailed, yet concise guide into the world of meditation and how it can help you deal with anxiety. Most importantly, it can help you deal with the most important symptoms that stem as a result of anxiety. You will learn about how meditation can become an effective, yet simple way in which you can improve your overall wellbeing and quality of life.

This book has been written for anyone who has had to deal with anxiety at any point in their lives. But in particular, it has been written for those who struggle with this condition despite their best efforts to harness their willpower and self-control. In addition, anyone who is interested in learning this topic with the intent to help a loved one will also find a great deal of information herein.

As a matter of fact, there are many prescribed methods available for dealing with anxiety: from aromatherapy, taking a walk, medical supplements, and the list just keeps growing. Anxiety may seem like a minute word to juggle around based on its primitive use in modern-day society. However, research has shown that it may not be as simple as people make it to be.

A whopping 40 million adults in the U.S. alone, aged above 18 years, suffer from anxiety disorders based on annual records.

Although highly treatable, only a rough 40% are able to get the form of treatment they seek. Rated as the most common mental disorder in the U.S. alone, the scale of its influence only proves to be wanting by the day.

Far from the aforementioned methods of dealing with it lies a soft-spoken method only mentioned by people not fully controlled by dogmatic sects: meditation. Meditation, though highly practiced within certain regions of the world, is highly demonized within some religious groups with the claims that it a pathway to demonic manifestation. Regardless, some people beg to differ based on the advantages that crop up after practicing various meditation techniques.

Receiving many converts on a day-to-day basis, many people get the chance to ascend from the many bodily issues that cloud them such as stress, heart conditions, anxiety, and even immunity. In addition, many meditation techniques only vouch for the wellbeing of oneself and others, which in turn eliminates the notion of its ungodliness. This book, therefore, delves into the different methods that can be used to battle anxiety, depression, and panic attacks.

So, let's jump right in and learn about how meditation can help you overcome anxiety, among other feelings of stress and worry. You have everything you need to overcome this condition. So, it is just a matter of learning strategies and guidelines which can help you achieve the health and wellbeing that you are seeking to achieve.

Chapter 1: Demystifying Anxiety

The introduction mentions the common misuse of the word anxiety among the public and the scale of its effects. Despite that, its social viewpoint remains subordinate as compared to other illnesses. People who suffer from it constantly experiencing dismissive comments such as 'just chill out' and 'just stop being nervous' without the understanding that it is more serious than what meets the eye.

Most people do not realize that anxiety is indeed as serious as depression. In a poll conducted in 2015 by the Anxiety and Depression Association of America, results showed that only half of the test group knew of a correlation between suicidal deaths and anxiety disorders. In addition to that, a staggering 70% of people reporting their suicidal history had an anxiety disorder that was diagnosable. It is dangerous, however, to ignore the relationship between suicide and anxiety.

While the effects of the disorder constantly wreak havoc, roughly one out of three people receive the treatment they need in order to regain the balance of their life. With that in mind, you can only begin to imagine how many cases remain shelved with no hope of seeking professional help.

Ignorance is not to blame for everything. So many hindrances occur that prevent people from accessing the sort of help they need. For instance, treating the disorder is not as cheap as it may appear. Professionals often require the affected to cough up large sums of money, which many people do not possess.

Societal norms greatly hinder the ordinary folks from seeking guidance when it comes to addressing their mental health. The notion that men are strong and those who show emotions are weak constantly continues to aggravate the males who in return opt to suffer in silence than talk about the issues surrounding them. As a result, men are almost 4 times prone to suffer from anxiety-related suicides.

In Kenya (a country that recently paid importance to the devastating male suicide rates), a whopping 330 men committed suicide in comparison to only 91 women in the year 2017, according to studies conducted by the World Health Organization. This figure alone underscores how detrimental sidelining the emotions of the male species can be. In a world that champions for the equality of all genders, there is no room for such stigma.

What Causes Anxiety?

Before looking into the reasons that fuel this disorder, it would only be fair to understand what it means: a feeling of unease that, in turn, stimulates feelings of fear, distress, and alertness. Anxiety is a normal occurring incident that affects most people occasionally. Not all people experience the same levels of anxiety, though. Although it may seem easy for some people to wade off the feelings that couple anxiety, some people often struggle and cannot seem to shake away the decapitating feelings that go in tandem with anxiety.

Anxiety can actually get to the point of messing with your daily routine. When this is the case, a person may have an anxiety disorder. In order to have a deeper understanding of it we will look at some of its triggers:

Health Complications

Nothing spells anxiety more than receiving bad news regarding one's health. For example, when a person receives a diagnosis of a chronic disease such as cancer or diabetes, stress is bound to ensue based on the many fears imposed on them by already victims. Because it is a personal encounter, it rubs off us more since nobody likes thinking of himself or herself as unwell.

Negative Thought Patterns

We are prisoners of our minds. Our mind, in turn, is responsible for the normal and healthy functioning of the body. Grounding our thought patterns with pessimism only return feelings of negativity, which eventually affect one's mental health. This is because the latter issue only contributes to mood and anxiety symptoms.

Too Much Caffeine

Epinephrine, one of the major hormones that catalyze the human natural response of fight or flight, increases when caffeine is present in the body. Anxiety is, therefore, common in people who indulge in many caffeinated drinks.

Social Events

Social events seem like 'the life' when presented to most people in general terms. However, being in a room with nothing but strangers might not be the best fun time for everyone. Many people dealing with anxiety carry around a haunting fear that the people they meet will judge them based on how they look or what they say. Therefore, social events do not really strike a deal with everyone. Anxious people, consequently, avoid making small talk or any form of interaction that may subsequently lead to their triggered anxiety.

Public Speaking

You have probably seen people become a nervous wreck when presented with the task of speaking in public; may it be in movies or in real life. In many cases, it is laughable not because of the act itself, but because of how people eventually react to it. The unserious nature of it is quite unreal. The lack of positive reinforcement from the audience is also subconsciously perceived as a joke.

Bullying

Behavioral responses of people, mostly children, exposed to bullying can give a clear picture of how it affects one's emotions and wellbeing. People who experience bullying in different settings often do not like spending time in the environment it occurs. The fear itself is distracting and throws one off their daily balance. Due to this response, the affected party may eventually end up underperforming. This only creates room for more anxiety and fear of social situations.

Bereavement

Sometimes we form close connections with other people that it throws us off balance when they pass away. Bereavement is associated with intense feelings of depression and grief, which may, later on, lead to anxiety. When a loved one dies, we face the fact that we will have to live the rest of our lives without their presence. Questions and fears of how to cope with grief often arise. Some people even believe that their lives will never be the same again. Such thoughts can drive one into anxiety.

Financial Problems

Money runs the world. We wake up every morning thinking of how we will get our next dollar. It has come to the point that for someone to be in a relationship they have to be well cashed. We question ourselves on a regular about our savings and debts.

Some of these worries definitely lead to anxiety. To make matters worse, we are bound to receive bills we never expected repeatedly.

These are just an example of some of the common triggers experienced by people. Personal triggers also come in to play and may vary between individuals. Because we all come across different types of societal conditioning, it makes it a little tricky to generalize everyone's trigger with those of the rest.

Signs You Have Anxiety Disorder

As mentioned before, anxiety is a normal part of everyday life. Every human being experiences anxiety at one or the other point of his or her life. Nonetheless, these events may take over one's life and cripple them from performing as a healthy member of society. Some of the common signs to look out for include:

Worrying Excessively

This is the most common sign that someone is suffering from general anxiety possibly leading into anxiety disorder. It should be noted that worrying is a normal part of the day-to-day human socialization. People with anxiety disorders have a tendency to worry too much. This worrying is intrusive to the point that it may end up crippling their daily running of things. This worry is mostly disproportionate if compared to what triggered it.

Being Restless

Restless people constantly feel like they are on edge. Research, however, shows that not everyone with anxiety will experience this symptom although doctors often inquire about it for diagnosis. It is one of the red flags. Being restless alone does not qualify one to be suffering from anxiety disorder.

Difficulty with Concentration

Have you ever been so anxious that you cannot seem to focus on a task? Do you feel that the more you try the more it fails? Well, studies have shown that anxiety indeed can interfere with the memory tasked to hold short-term information, the working memory. This explains the unusual drop in performance experienced by people who are victims of anxiety. People who experience high levels of anxiety have most trouble concentrating on their daily routine as well as other tasks.

If you suffer from difficulty with concentration, on the other hand, it may not essentially act as enough evidence to prove that one suffers from anxiety. It may be a sign of other conditions that plague the human race such as attention deficit disorder.

Muscle Tension

Although the direct correlation is not fully graspable yet, having tense muscles on a constant is highly linked to having anxiety. The previous statement serves as proof that the link between these two has yet to be established. Confusion arises because it is difficult to tell whether having tense muscles induces more anxiety or vice versa. It is also possible that a third cause comes in play to link these two.

All the same, the treatment of muscle tension has repeatedly served as proof that it helps tame feelings of worry and distress.

Panic Attacks

People who suffer from panic attacks often experience an intensified feeling of crippling fear. Associated with it are panic disorders that lie under the family of anxiety disorders. The affected often experience intensified heartrates, nausea, and fear of the unknown, sweating and shaking as well as difficulty breathing.

We all experience panic attacks at one point in our lives. We do not all suffer from panic disorders, though. Only a small percentage of people experience it with enough frequency to qualify as victims of panic disorders.

Insomnia

Everybody likes a good night's sleep. Not everyone gets to have the pleasure of having it as good as expected. People who suffer from anxiety disorder are unfortunate enough to fall into this category. In fact, a common problem aired by them is having trouble sleeping and waking up at odd hours of the night with the inability to go back to their forty winks.

Just like muscle tension, researchers have found it hard to establish whether insomnia causes anxiety, vice versa or both. An important point to note is that, when the prime causes of anxiety disorder are treated, the sleep patterns usually go back to normal as well.

The Five Types of Anxiety Disorders

It is a normal occurrence to be anxious just as mentioned earlier. The way this world works, it would be almost impossible not to have feelings of anxiety repeatedly. We are predisposed to engage ourselves in activities that may give rise to feelings of anxiety: doing exams, asking someone out for a date, making important decisions among others.

Anxiety disorders come in different shapes and forms. The term anxiety disorder only serves as an umbrella term to cover the different conditions under the scope of the term:

Social Phobias (Social Anxiety Disorder)

For socially anxious people, everyday situations can get out of hand in mere seconds. This group of people is extremely self-conscious and fear judgment and scrutiny from other individuals. This phobia links itself to only specific situations:

- Fear of public speaking
- Having meals in front of people
- In extreme cases, others experience it in slight exposure to other people

In the event that you experience these kinds of symptoms, you might actually be suffering from social anxiety.

Generalized Anxiety Disorder (GAD)

Generalized Anxiety Disorder has the tendency of making the victims feel unfounded worry as well as the lingering feeling that something negative is about to happen. Often, these feelings come in excessive proportions and are mostly unrealistic.

Post-Traumatic Stress Disorder (PTSD)

Contrary to popular belief, PTSD does not only affect soldiers and prisoners of war. This anxiety disorder comes about when someone goes through adverse conditions that may terrify or cause physical harm to him or her. A couple of traumatic events can easily lead one to post-traumatic stress disorder: various accidents, natural or synthetic disasters and violence imposed on them. Three symptoms generally characterize PTSD:

- Flashbacks, nightmares, and vivid recollections of the events that lead to the current state.

- Having insomnia coupled with the inability to concentrate as well as amplified feelings of anger and irritation.

- Heavy avoidance of places, things or activities that serve as a constant reminder of the traumatic event.

Panic Disorder

People who suffer from panic disorders always have terror knocking at their doors on a constant. The affected parties also experience sweating, heavy palpitations (usually irregular) and chest pains. In addition, none of these episodes comes with a warning and the fear of another attack only adds the magnitude of the panic. In extreme cases, victims may experience a choking sensation and symptoms that they may be having a heart attack.

Obsessive-Compulsive Disorder (OCD)

When the term OCD comes up, many people often characterize it with the washing of hands and turning on and off lights. However, to many people, many things are a mystery about people who suffer from OCD. OCD has the characteristic of repetitive actions and thought patterns (obsessions) that recur. Some of the obsessions are:

- The fear of contamination from germs
- Unwelcome thoughts of harm, religion, or sex
- Thoughts of aggression towards the self or other parties
- Arranging thing is perfect symmetry

Some of these repetitive actions may be arranging things in a specific way, excessive urge to clean the surroundings and wash hands, counting and checking things repeatedly to confirm if they are in order.

There is no way, for certain, to be able to tell when or how someone will develop an anxiety disorder. Gladly, there are steps present, which can help reduce or alleviate the symptoms. Contained in this book are some of these steps.

Chapter 2: What is Meditation?

In the previous chapter, we took a look at anxiety and the ripple effect it has on our daily routine. As some of you have discovered, anxiety is not a small deal. Some people's lives come to a grinding halt because of this menace and it continues to do so on a daily basis. The previous chapter also gives light (although not expounded) about some techniques that can come in handy when battling anxiety. Meditation, although not mentioned, happens to be one of these handy techniques.

To many people, the technique appears as somewhat vague and difficult to grasp without giving it a bit of time to see the results. To some, the battle with the fleeting mind only discourages them from taking a step further to calm the mind. To others, religious dogma stands in their way. Some folks have chosen to embrace the practice and report numerous benefits, some even taking up journeys to go and meditate in every known meditation center. It is completely okay to belong to any of these groups because the practice in itself requires a lot of dedication and open-mindedness without which the practice may appear boring or unfruitful. It is a practice for a reason!

Yet, what is this phenomenon called "meditation"? Meditation is a practice that involves the application of various techniques such as breathing and mindfulness in order to achieve a calm mental state and train focus and attention. The main purpose of the practice is to help you observe your feelings and emotions without judgment with the benefit that you will get to understand them well. Therefore, meditation does not make you a holy person or a different person but it has the potential to if you wish to take the path.

What is not meditation? Meditation is not a practice meant to make you high or zone out or even have bizarre experiences. Many people carry this notion around with them. It would be a good idea to dispel some of these thoughts before getting yourself to start the practice lest you feel deceived. Meditation is an avenue to train your mind in awareness.

History of Meditation

Whether you are new to the concept or whether you are already a guru about to reach enlightenment, learning about the history of this practice is very important. Wall art in India that shows people seated in the meditation pose with closed eyes appeared approximately 5,000 to 3,500 BC serve as one of the oldest documented proof of the practice. Even so, the oldest written records of the practice trace back to the Vedas in 1,500 BC. Nevertheless, for them to write it down, the practice passed down orally for over centuries.

Anciently, meditation was a practice of the religious and practitioners of asceticism. These people abandoned all the pleasures of the world to transcend themselves over life's limitations.

Around the 6th Century BC, the Buddha Siddhartha Gautama who was a prince at the time decided to abandon the palace and find enlightenment. He disposed himself to the best yogis he could find in his region but was still not satisfied by the outcome of his results. He decided to go into the forest, sit under a tree, and meditate until he achieved what he direly craved. He was fruitful enough to discover his own technique of meditation and achieve enlightenment. He spent the rest of his life serving people and teaching them this practice. The spread of Buddhism ensued over the next centuries and its lineages are some of the most famous modes of meditation in the West.

Confucianism, Taoism, and Jainism received birth in the same Century that Buddha existed but have their own approach towards the meditation practice. Confucianism focusses more on morality, Taoism with cosmic life and Jainism on self-discipline, non-violence, and purification of the self. Although still practiced today, they do not much the popularity of Yoga and Buddhism outside of their home countries.

The cultural influence propagated by Alexander the Great's military activities from 327 to 325 BC brought Indians and Greek philosophers in touch. Under the influence of yogis and sages, the Greek philosophers were able to form their own version of meditation-navel gazing. Popularly known as omphaloskepsis, it was a common practice among philosophers to assist them in their philosophical thoughts. This meditation technique did not hold for so long as other philosophers such as Plotinus and Philo of Alexandria developed other methods that dealt with concentration. Moreover, the Christian crusades that dominated the West eventually snuffed out these traditions until later on in the 20th Century.

Mystics from the Christian pool also developed their own form of meditation. Its characteristics were the contemplation of God and repetitions of special words or phrases that held divine meaning. A well-known form of meditation is the Jesus Prayer, which sprouted in Greece between the 10th and 14th Century. According to historian speculations, their influence of meditation occurred when a group of Christians ran into the Indians and the Sufis. Benedictine monks are responsible for the further development of Christian meditation.

While visiting China, Dosho a Japanese monk discovered the art of Zen and introduced the practice into his country when he returned. He also opened the first meditation hall. The practice gained popularity in the 8th Century with Japan, Korea, and Vietnam adopting the practice.

The mystics of Islam, popularly known as the Sufis, introduced a practice of meditation that revolved around gazing, mantras and breathing. They received some of their influence from Indian traditions. The main purpose of their meditation practice is to have a connection with God. In Turkey today, the Sufi swirl (also developed by them) is still noticeable.

Meditation continued to develop and grow during the middle Ages as religious traditions masked in forms of prayers like the Jewish meditation. Meditation teachings saw their popularity in the midst of Western cultures during this time. Meditation has been able to traverse many narrow pathways and reach the ears of many since then.

Science was able to tap into the resource of meditation in the 1930's. James Funderburk, a student of the Himalayan Institute of Yoga Science, made studies of scientific research on meditation possible in 1977. He was a student of Swami Rama, one of the first yogis studied by scientists from the West. Under scientific observation in the 60's, Swami Rama displayed his ability to control his blood pressure, body temperature and heartbeat voluntarily. Among other things, he also displaced the ability to:

- Produce delta, alpha, gamma, and theta brain waves on-demand.

- Remain environmentally conscious while still in deep sleep.

- Manipulate his heartbeat while assuming a motionless pose and stopping his heart for a couple of seconds.

- Generate different skin temperatures on different sides of his hand.

This led to the popularization of scientific studies on meditation over the next five decades. As the quality of machines increased, the quality of these findings also increased. Although meditation (during this time) was highly referred to as a religious practice, some of these feats set in motion the end of this belief. Meditation is a form of healthcare thanks to this.

Presently, the practice of meditation is experiencing secular and mainstream recognition, mostly to influence wellness of mind and body. This does not mean that spiritual meditation has seen its end. The practice is still in motion. However, it is the value of wellness still acts as the biggest attractor to the practice of meditation. This is just an overview of how the practice spread.

Forms of Meditation

Mindfulness Meditation

This is the practice of being present fully –that is not focusing on the past or future. This is the art of being contemporaneous and being present with your thoughts. This means we ought to be aware and not reactive – that is to observe what we do and where we are and not react to what is going on around us. This is in essence, mindfulness. Mindful meditation can usually be practiced anywhere. However, most people prefer to sit with their eyes closed while focusing on their breathing. If you so wish, however, you can be mindful as you walk, drink a cup of tea, work or relax. When practicing this, one observes their emotions and thoughts from a non-judgmental point of view.

Guided Meditation

This type of meditation involves visualization and imagery in which one visualizes an object or image of either shape, color, a saintly person, a god, or a goddess, or even a place that makes you feel relaxed. This meditation is referred to as 'guided' as you have a teacher or guide that leads the process. In order to induce calmness in your space, it is advisable to use as many senses as possible: sight, hearing, touch, smell, and taste.

Transcendental Meditation

This is a simple technique in which one has a personally assigned mantra, such as a sound, word, or phrase is repeated in a specific manner. This type of meditation is practiced twice a day for twenty minutes in each session. Its goal is to achieve inner peace without effort or concentration by allowing you to settle inwards to an intense state of relaxation and rest.

Vipassana Meditation

Taught in the tradition of Sayagi U Ba Khin, Vipassana aims to see things as they are and not as we would like them to be. It was taught in India nearly 25 Centuries ago and is said to have been the form of meditation practiced by Gautama the Buddha. Mindfulness Meditation, from the United States, has roots in this practice.

The essence of Vipassana is self-transformation through self-observation. This phenomenon is accomplished by observing different sensations on the physical aspect of the body in order to forge a strong connection between mind and body. This connection generates a balanced mind full of love and compassion.

Vipassana in this tradition is taught over a ten-day course where students are expected to observe a set of five precepts throughout the course including abstaining from lies, stealing, intoxicants, sexual activity and killing any species.

Mētta Meditation

This is also known as loving-kindness meditation as it is the practice of sharing one's merits and directing well wishes of happiness, peace, and harmony to others. It is a practice that happens after Vipassana and Mindful Meditations.

The usual practice happens when one is in a calm and relaxed state and after a few breaths, one will slowly and steadily repeat words of good wishes of happiness, peace, and harmony to oneself and then later directing it to other people they may wish and visualize. The mediation usually ends with the universal mantra "May All Beings Be Happy."

Chakra Meditation

The spiritual power and energy centers present in the human body are chakras. There are seven chakras in total, and they are all located at different points in the body: crown chakra, third eye chakra, the throat chakra, the heart chakra, the navel chakra, the sacral chakra, and the root chakra. The practice, therefore, involves bringing oneness by unblocking the chakras.

The use of crystals and incense is very common in this practice as it helps in concentrating on the different chakras present. Sometimes, visualizing a color and its corresponding chakra while meditating is another common technique. Yes, chakras do have colors.

Yoga Meditation

Known to be one of the most popular forms of meditation, yoga gets its roots from ancient India. There are eight known types of yoga: Vinyasa, Iyengar, Power, Bikram, Jivamukti, Ashtanga, Sivananda and Yin yoga. All these types have the characteristic of breathing exercises while trying to achieve different postures. The practice promotes calmness and flexibility.

Due to the different types of techniques available, it is advisable to do ample research and find whichever type suits you, depending on any type of physical ailment that might come in the way.

Why People Meditate

There are diverse reasons why people meditate. These are just as diverse as the types of meditation we have presented. The benefits in themselves are not kept as secret. The evidence seen is from the many people who adopt the practice and stick to it. Most people who attempt to sell the idea of meditation do so by convincing people that it is practices by happy and successful to cope with everyday life. Repeatedly, it receives mentions to be the future of wellness due to the positive impacts presented by the thousands of studies undertaken.

Here are some of the common reasons why people meditate:

To Relax

It is a major reason why people meditate. It is easy to understand that most people do not want the effects of the minor obstacles that repeatedly present themselves. Often when faced with an obstacle, our bodies react with the "fight-or-flight" response, an aversion technique well known to the mind. For a meditator, the case is different; the body responds with the "relaxation response" which is the complete opposite of fight-or-flight.

Through meditation, one has the ability to face anxiety and restore the feeling of calm. This way, everyday obstacles do not hinder your daily performance or targets. In addition, the relaxation response maintains the normal functioning of our mental activity, blood pressure, and heart rate.

Beating Anxiety

We have the tendency of focusing our attention on the negative things that might decide to take place-but often never happen. From experience, these mental escapades completely take our attention away from the task at hand causing ourselves a lot of bodily and sometimes physical stress.

Research has it that meditation is a good avenue to direct your anxiety. It is of great use to victims of generalized anxiety as well. It helps them alleviate worries, irritability, and dwindling sleep patterns.

To Connect with Self and Others

With the mindset of living in the present and self-awareness, the art of meditation brings awareness to your true nature. By constantly observing ourselves, we can easily get to understand the deeper states of our mind and the feelings that go in tandem with them. By getting to experience who we are in this subtle nature, we develop a deeper understanding of how our triggers work. Eventually, one begins to experience a state of calm and tranquility that gives us a deeper and healthier connection with oneself.

As the old saying goes "you cannot love others if you do not love yourself". Consequently, building self-awareness through this art, we allow ourselves to become empathetic towards other people. Our relationships with other people take a turn for the better. In addition, grudges meet their end quickly because of the built-in understanding of others through self.

To Boost Attention Span

Meditation can easily be termed as weightlifting for the mind. By focusing on different objects such as the breath, the endurance, and strength of the mind increases. The pre-frontal cortex is stimulated every time a person is meditating.

Practitioners of meditation have long discovered that by focusing on one's breath or an object for a stipulated amount of time, the attention span increases significantly. A study conducted on human resource workers showed that those who practiced meditation could focus on a task for longer than those who do not practice. Moreover, they could account for every detail of their task better as compared to their peers who did not take up the practice. Meditation is also a very useful tool to reduce unwanted mental patterns such as mind wandering and worrying.

To Get Better Sleep

Getting a good night's rest means you can face the next day with a tire-free and relaxed body and mind. Since each of us might have experienced insomnia at one time of our lives, it would not be difficult to relate to how missing a good night's sleep can really interrupt the events of the following day.

Sleep is very important for the running of cognitive functions. Meditation has a link to the increase of deep sleep (REM sleep) through the secretion of melatonin often referred to as the sleep hormone. A skilled meditator knows what to do to fight the restless mind that often leads to sleep deprivation. In addition, meditation has the power to release tension hence relax your body thus leaving you in a better state to fall asleep.

To Battle Addictions

Vipassana meditation is practiced by hundreds of thousands of people worldwide. There is a strong belief that addictions are not caused by the drug themselves but by the bodily sensations that are aroused when indulging in a drug.

Through the mental discipline, self-awareness, and self-control that develops through various meditation practices, the breaking of dependencies is easy or accelerated. The practice in itself makes it easy for practitioners to redirect their attention, control their impulses and get a better understanding of the triggers that lead to their addictive behavior.

Food cravings may as well come to a grinding halt through the practice of meditation. Emotions that get out of control can induce binge eating. Meditation can help one get a grip on emotions in such a manner that cravings can be fully controlled.

To Relieve Pain

Based on clinical experiments, mindfulness meditation proves to reduce 57% of chronic pain. The human brain has the capacity to release a natural pain reliever called endorphins, which reduces inflammations. After achieving a deep state of mind and shifting your attention to other sensations, you prevent your body from excreting more stress hormones.

Studies have shown that the section of the mind known to control pain shows more activity in meditators. Reports also show that they have little sensitivity to levels of pain. The same cause of pain experienced by meditators and non-meditators is the same. Meditators, however, show to handle the pain more efficiently to the extent of experiencing reduced pain.

It Is Free

Unlike many practices, the art of meditation does not require you to spend any money in order for you to experience the benefits it offers. All you have to do is sit down in the meditation pose (or any other comfortable position) and watch your anxiety, anger, grief, or pain go away. People living in rural areas do not have to travel for long distances to the city to see a physician anymore. Why? You are your own physician! As long as meditation can cure it, all you need is to stay put and meditate.

The list of reasons why people meditate is endless. Above are just some of the major reasons that drive individuals to be part of the practice. The bottom line remains that people mostly meditate to feel good.

Why People Do Not Meditate

It would be fair, in my opinion, to cover some of the reasons why people do not seem to like or appreciate the practice. It would also be fair to understand that most people do not know that they are more than what they see on the physical. They might intellectually understand this but not at the experiential level. It is okay if you do not want anything to do with the practice; not everything is for everyone. However, it would be unfair to demonize something without giving it a fair trial.

Quieting the Mind

Some people begin the practice with a lot of expectations and set timeframes that they will use to mark their achievements. This kind of attitude only makes the mind busier as you cannot shake off the thoughts of your 'impending successes'. Considering the human mind experiences an average of 60,000 thoughts every 24 hours, it would be pointless to try to quiet the mind. You cannot stop your thoughts from coming and going; this is the nature of the mind.

Starting fights with the mind will only make the thought patterns stronger leading to agitation. There is no active fighting involved but only observation. By engaging more in the practice, then, your thoughts will start to subside.

What is the Point?

Many people associate meditation with passing fads that do not make sense. Who would blame them? So many things crop up on daily that everyone would suggest you try. From the history of meditation covered above, it is clear that the practice has traversed centuries. Multitudes of people have sought the practice for peace, happiness, and even mental control. The state of your mind influences your success. When you access your attention, you have good access to your mind.

So, what is the point of meditation? Well, to build your attention. By doing this, we are able to pay close attention to the positive things in our lives and give none to the ones that pull us down. This way, we train ourselves not to focus on stress and allow ourselves to experience peace and contentment.

Lack of Time

Someone who I hold dearly once told me, "the people who say they do not have time to meditate should be the ones meditating the most". Think about it. People who claim to be constantly busy have so many things clouding their minds that are bound to lead their minds to overdrive. Are you one of these people? If so, meditation should be your medication.

A good way to start would be to have a record of the unproductive times you have during the day. If you spend an hour daily watching television, spending a quarter of that time meditating would be ideal to start your journey. Some people conclude that after beginning meditation, they get more time in their lives. Now that the mental chaff starts clearing, you can go about your day with clarity.

It is Spiritual

As much as meditation sprouts from religious backgrounds for spiritual goals, its practice is mostly a body-mind exercise as essentially carried out by Western nations. Muslims, Christians and even Agnostics can carry out this practice without the fear of it infringing on your religious standpoint.

Some people may decide to perform special rituals or wear specific clothes before meditating. It is important to note that these are just personal preferences and people who do this find the practices helpful in their meditation. You are free to omit whatever practice you do not deem fit and carry on with whatever feels beneficial. If you are wary about the repetition of words, it is totally fine. Many methods available do not require any form of verbalization.

I Do Not Need an Escape

First, meditation is nothing like an escape. On the contrary, it only makes you face the bitter reality of life-but with a clear mind. If this was the foundation of your meditation and it did not work out as well, you now probably have an idea why. For you to be able to escape from something, you need a form of distraction or intoxication. Meditation is neither of those. Meditation only heightens awareness. People who practice meditation also go through problems. The only difference is that they are able to face these problems in a peaceful conscious state.

If someone decided to use the practice to run away from their problems and eventually ends up not working, the blame is on the person, not on meditation. Money does not create evil people but amplifies the evil that is in people. The same principle applies here.

It Is a Selfish Act

To some, the idea of sitting by oneself to attain peace within seems to be very selfish. "Why not share the peace with others?" they might ask. Let us look at it differently. It is a common thing to say that you cannot love someone if you do not love yourself. Again, you cannot spread peace if you do not have it. Easy, right?

Meditation is just another way to spend time with yourself just like reading a book or listening to your favorite album. If it was selfish, things like sleeping, grooming and self-pleasures should also hold the same ground. The results may not be tangible but your experience and that of those who experience you will be different.

It Has No Space for Emotions

While this may be true to some point, it is also not the case. Meditation does have space for your emotions it just does not advocate for you to act on them without foresight. The idea behind it is to free you from the bondage of mental slavery. In addition, we are all slaves to our emotions, right? What is so bad about inner freedom?

Everybody is bound to experience strong emotions sometime. Meditation will only make you less reactive to these emotions as you will be working from a deeper understanding of oneself and others.

It is Boring

Humph! You can dispel this reason with only one word: attitude! If someone approaches the practice with the mentality of fun and games, qualms and pains will meet you instead. It is understandable that in this modern world, it is so easy to get satisfaction from anything that meditation would not seem like a go to the source.

Many people from different lifestyles have found it important to spare a bit of time to meditate on a daily basis. In other cases, people have abandoned everything they own and know to spend their whole lives meditating. It comes to question what they must have experienced to make this 'extreme' decision. A good example is the Buddha who abandoned his life as a prince (and all the earthly pleasures that come with the status) and spent his whole life meditating under a tree.

The Results Take Years

The levels of benefits reaped by meditation are different compared to how you take on the practice. If you do it for a very little duration of time on a daily basis your results are bound to take a bit longer compared to someone who does three hours a day. This does not mean that you should immediately leap to doing four hours a day to reap better benefits- it may discourage you and bar you from seeing the practice as it is- a practice.

Research has shown that eight weeks of repetitive practice can hone amazing mental and physical benefits. A few weeks is all you need to notice the benefits. If you are on the path of enlightenment, however, you will require a lot of time to achieve this compared to someone looking for health and mental balance.

Tips to Better Meditation

For someone to have a good meditation experience, a couple of things may need comprehension. Meditation is a fun activity that may not be so when a couple of things remain unaddressed especially to new practitioners.

The Mind Will Wander

Most people claim that their first meditation experience might have been the worst because of the monkey mind we all possess (it keeps jumping from one situation to the next). This alone has seen many new practitioners of the practice throw in the towel.

It is normal for the mind to wander- this has been the habit pattern of the mind since birth. When you notice that your mind has started to wander, getting frustrated will not make it not wander. Instead, just refocus your mind on whatever you were initially doing while keeping a balanced mind. This way with enough practice, you will be able to notice the habit patterns of the mind and acquire a firm grip of it as well.

Strategies for Successful Meditation

Make Yourself Comfortable

Sitting in the meditation pose may not be the most comfortable position for a new practitioner to try out as it may result in backaches. Sitting on a couch or a cushion can help mitigate this meditation discourager. Some practices even allow you to lie down as long as you do not fall asleep. In most cases, it is advisable not to lie down because one is highly prone to fall asleep.

Find out the Practice for You

Through many social interactions, you get to find out that a huge number of people get into the practice without proper research on which technique will suit them most. They just do whatever their friends say or seem familiar. One needs to understand that different types of practices have different results. Being familiar with the background of a technique is very important to avoid being misled.

Find a Nice Environment

Creating a nice and serene place to practice meditation can really boost one in the discipline. This place needs to be quiet and far from distractions with clean air. Due to the current state of industrialization, it may be difficult to find a quiet place- that should not break your spirit. It is possible to invest in very cheap earplugs that do the trick and cost not more than 2 dollars. A serene environment aids in improving concentration and can transform your meditation experience.

Have a Gradual Start

If it is your first time, meditating for 2 hours straight does not really seem reasonable, does it? It is not a perfect-it is a practice. The journey of meditation happens to be more important than the destination. Starting with 10 minutes, slowly build up with small increments. That seems like quite the ideal idea. Setting high standards for yourself might only lead you to discouragement, leading you not to give the practice a good try.

Guided Meditation

Many guided meditations exist on the internet. They exist in many tastes and preferences and can be helpful for anyone having a hard time getting themselves to meditate. From YouTube to diverse apps, guided meditation audios are all over.

Pick a Good Time

It is not advisable to meditate immediately after eating to your fill. Neither is it advisable to try it before bed when you are sleepy. Instead, pick a time that fits well with your schedule. You do not have to meditate every morning just because your friend does it. Anytime is a perfect time to meditate.

Your Breath Is Your Anchor

When your fleeting mind keeps wandering, you can use your breath as an anchor. Do not be discouraged or drawn in too much by the fantasies. Bring back your focus to your breath and try to keep it there if you have trouble concentrating. In due time, you will notice you can observe your breath for longer periods. This is bound to improve your concentration.

Don't Judge the Practice

If you have decided to take a leap and try out meditation, it would be a good idea to let go of all judgments that cloud your mind about the practice. Judging something and practicing it at the same time may not lead to good results, as you have not fully surrendered yourself to the technique. Instead of approaching meditation with judgment, do some research about it and its ethical standing before attempting the practice. It would also be advisable to ask a friend about it. They might give you important insight.

It is without a doubt that if the above are observed you are sure to have a good meditation experience. Fully preparing yourself physically and mentally for something new is also important. Try not to rush into something you do not comprehend.

One last thing, trying it in groups (especially Metta meditators) can be a good boost for people who have trouble doing it alone. You never know what you can learn from others.

Chapter 3: Getting Started

The last chapter covered some of the fundamentals that are needed for the proper comprehension of meditation right before adopting the practice. Most people who report having quit meditation also expressed complaints that stem from the lack of understanding of some of these concepts. I, therefore, advise you to read it carefully before proceeding.

In this chapter, we will look into some of the basic ways to start the practice of meditation. We will look at some of the known forms of meditation that would serve as a good starting point, systematically. These are breathing, counting and mindfulness meditation. Remember, if you feel like it might be tricky doing it on your own, you can always seek the assistance of guided meditations and group settings.

The great meditators of the past discovered a connection between external realities and our body and mind. They discovered that we can live a life of higher consciousness by being able to observe what we feel within while still paying attention to without. They discovered that our thoughts and emotions could be our slaves contrary to what is the reality.

To notice how your emotions, shift, observe your breath. When we relax, our breathing is regulated and deep while fast when we experience excitement. With this in mind, the Buddhists discovered that as our breathing can alter our state of mind the same way our state of mind shifts our breathing. In return, this means that if we learn to breathe correctly, we have the power to do away with many unpleasant feelings that torment us on a daily basis.

The negative emotions that we experience coupled with the negative effects they bring about to deal with a lot of damage to our personal and emotional growth. By learning to do away with these self-inflicted vices, we allow ourselves to grow in greater proportions in comparison to people who do not heed this advice. With a calm and clear mind, we make better decisions and play a good fit as a functioning member of society. Before getting into the actual first practice, it would be nice to learn the correct method of breathing.

The natural way our body is supposed to breathe is the abdominal breathing method. At first, it may appear unnatural but this is indeed the natural way for our bodies to breathe. From conception up until a point after birth, this is how our bodies breathe. However, as our age progress, we diverge from this mode of breathing and start breathing while expanding the chest. This newly adopted method only causes the mind to be in a state of anxiety. One should carry out abdominal breathing in this method:

- Assuming you are in a comfortable sitting position, keep an upright posture with your feet apart and touching the ground.

- Place your hands (with the thumbs touching) against the lower section of your belly and let them form a rainbow arc.

- Keeping your chin tucked, press your tongue behind the upper row of teeth. Keep the eyes open and do not stare into any objects.

- Gently, inhale. As you exhale, push out the lower belly and feel the air rush out. Do not completely fill your belly with air; having it three quarters filled is sufficient.

- The exhaling should be equally gentle. It occurs through the nose. Push in your belly to symbolize squeezing out the air. Each step should last you at most 4 seconds each for uniformity.

As aforementioned, it may seem strange to breathe in coordination with the belly for beginners. This gets better and starts to feel more natural with more practice. Furthermore, it is the natural way to breathe.

Beginner Breathing

First, find a good sitting position that will not interfere with the process. You can use the meditation pose or sit on a chair with your hands resting on the sides and a straightened back. Do not get too comfortable though- you might 'meditate' until the next morning.

Minimize any form of distraction that can take your away attention from the meditation process. Some of these things may be a mobile phone, flashing lights, kids looking for your attention, your pet or even the weather. Find out if you should keep warm or wear loose fitted clothes before you start meditating. You may wish to close your eyes or even focus on a specific spot or object in your surroundings.

Once you are seated and comfortable with your eyes closed (or open), relax your muscles and start observing your breath. Do not try to change anything about it. The body knows the amount of air it requires. Just observe your nostrils as air flows naturally through them-in and out. The air may be cool, warm, or itchy. Every feeling is the right feeling- just observe without any judgment.

Stray thoughts may come in droves but do not hate yourself or form any resentment towards them. Just observe how your mind has the tendency of wandering and try to bring back your thoughts to breathe observation. Keep breathing and keep going deeper. Notice how the sounds around you keep drowning the deeper you take your attention into your breathing.

If stray thoughts keep recurring, notice the pattern of these thoughts. Notice what they are about, what they mostly consist of and if they are from the past or present. Bring your attention back to your breathing and continue observing your breath. At first, it may even be difficult to observe two breaths before the mind wanders. This is totally fine as it is part of the journey. Keep noticing without judgment.

Bodily distractions often come into play when meditating. Some common ones are itching, discomfort or even pain. Sometimes, different sets of emotions may arise such as sorrow or joy but they are impermanent-whatever they are. This should not stop you from the process. Simply observe what they are without judgment and accept whatever stories come up. Then, slowly guide yourself back to observing your breathing.

When your time runs out, bring back your attention to your body and to your surroundings. Notice how relaxed your mind is and how your breath remains the same as you open your eyes. Repeat this daily and cultivate the practice before increasing your time. You are bound to see results.

Mindful Walking Meditation

This technique comes in handy for people who are always on the move or cannot get themselves to sit and meditate. In fact, its efficiency stems from the fact that you do not need to add another routine to your daily activities to make it work. All you have to do is walk mindfully. You can always walk mindfully as you carry on with your normal routine. This practice helps to cultivate a lot of awareness as one observes within while facing the distractions of life.

It would be advisable to choose an appropriate place where you are likely to get fewer distractions as well as have good walking space. Begin with a stationary, upright position. Feel the weight of your body on your feet. You have the freedom to place your hands behind, either resting on your sides or even clasped around your chest- whatever feels comfortable. As you do this, remain relaxed and observe whatever sensations you feel objective.

Start walking using short slow steps and pay attention to the feelings that arise and pass on your feet. These feelings can vary from pain, pressure, heat or even heaviness. There is no right or wrong feeling to experience. All you have to do is observe them as they arise and pass. In this practice, the feelings one encounters as they walk are the anchor unlike in breathing meditation.

Keep walking and pay close attention to the sensations experienced on your feet as you make every step. As your foot rises and as it falls back to the ground, what do you feel? After making nonjudgmental observations, keep walking towards the chosen destination while keeping a natural and relaxed posture. When you get to the end of the walk, stand for a couple of seconds, and observe what your body feels. Before turning, center your attention back to your feet and start walking slowly again.

If the initial pace is chosen does not seem to suit the experience, feel free to switch it up a bit to the level of your comfort. You might find that walking fast works better for you! Notice how impermanent the walk is; how you keep going back and forth in the same path. You may also notice how impermanent the sensations that occur as you walk are. Just simply observe and keep practicing.

In comparison to beginner breathing, the mind is bound to wander even when doing mindful walking. This is totally fine. Noticing that your mind has wandered is half the journey. You, however, need to refocus your attention back to the next step gradually. If you notice your mind spent twenty minutes wandering, that is still fine. The fact that you noticed and refocused yourself is the most important part. Oh, and keep your eyes open!

Counting Meditation

Counting meditation is exactly as it sounds. You just need to be relaxed with your eyes closed and count up to the desired number. Ridiculous? I think not! Do you remember when we talked about the use of anchors? In this case, the numbers are your anchor. Anytime the mind decides to drift away, slowly bring back your attention to where you left off and continue counting. A practice like this can really do wonders for your attention span. Remember to observe with no judgment.

If the real intention is present when performing this practice, you will notice the intensity of the thought patterns subsides. Your thoughts will go in tandem with the counting. The more you learn to bring back your mind to focus, the more your mind detaches itself from its habitual patterns. Self-awareness develops.

These are just some of the basic meditation techniques that serve as great starters for a new meditator. If you grasp either one of these first, transitioning to the rest of the techniques taught in this book will be easy as one, two, and three.

Chapter 4: Dealing with Stress

Stress, however unpleasant, is a normal reaction that occurs in our body and is sometimes beneficial. It is the body's response to changes that are occurring and require adjustment or response. These responses can be physical, mental, or emotional. As a normal part of life, stress can be triggered by everyday things around us such as our environment, our thoughts, and our body. These stressors can either be positive such as getting married or negative such as getting fired from job. The more stressors you experience, the more load you are likely to feel on your nervous system. Simply put, stress can be defined as the feeling we get when we're overwhelmed and struggling to cope with demands. Even so, anything that poses a threat or challenge, real or perceived, causes stress.

Stress acts as an indicator of danger and is thus beneficial for our survival. This is where the 'fight or flight' response comes to play. Stress flushes our body systems with hormones to help us confront or evade danger by telling us when and how to react to danger. This is the fight or flight mechanism and is the reason stress can be defined as the body's natural defense against danger. This mechanism always fuels a physical reaction –that is to either get away from the situation or stay and fight the stressor. Following the flush of hormones, our bodies tend to produce larger quantities of chemicals and hormones such as adrenaline, cortisol, and noradrenaline that in turn cause a specific response in the body such as increased heart rate, alertness, sweating and muscle preparedness all which will aid the final response of fight or flight.

Stress is helpful and can be a motivator; in this context it is referred to as eustress –that is positive stress that keeps us productive and on the go. In many cases, it helps save our lives by helping us react in a way to stop or prevent danger, for example, jerking off the road when you see a car coming your way. In other cases, it serves as a motivator, for instance, helping you focus on a project that's due or keeping you on guard during a presentation or speech. We all experience and go through stress differently but like everything else, too much of it is dangerous and can lead to health problems.

Effects of Chronic Stress

Our nervous systems are not good at distinguishing between physical and emotional threats. For instance, your body cannot distinguish between the stressed caused by an exam or a robber in front of you. In either case, your body is likely to give off the same reaction. The more your stress systems are activated the easier you can be triggered and the harder it is to get out of a state of constant stress. This is referred to as chronic stress and is the most harmful form of stress- it goes on for long periods and occurs when one never sees the end to a stressor and stops finding solutions.

This is even more common in today's demanding society. This leads us to get used to it and become unnoticeable as it makes up part of our personalities. Nowadays, our bodies are in a constant heightened state of stress, which more often than not leads to serious health problems. Stress disrupts almost all of one's body systems and can rewire the brain causing one to be vulnerable to anxiety, depression, other mental illnesses and in other cases, it can cause heart attacks, strokes, violent actions, and suicide.

While stress is usually a short-term experience of your body's reaction to a trigger, anxiety is a sustained mental disorder that is triggered by prolonged periods of stress. Anxiety does not usually fade away once the stressor is evaded, on the contrary, it stays for long and can cause impairment and damage to areas of functioning such as societal involvement and one's occupational responsibilities.

Signs and Symptoms of Chronic Stress

It is important to understand and be aware of the common signs of stress overload as you may get used to indulging in stressful situations and not pay much attention to the damage it's causing to your health and wellbeing.

Emotional Signs and Symptoms

- Feeling overwhelmed

- Agitation and anxiety

- Anger, mood swings and feeling irritable

- Isolation and loneliness

- Irritability

- Forgetfulness

- Anger

- Restlessness

- Insecurity

- Fatigue

- Sadness and depression

- Rise of mental or emotional health problems

Cognitive Signs and Symptoms

- Racing thoughts

- Poor judgment

- Memory problems

- Anxious thoughts

- Constant worrying

- Pessimism and negativity

- Concentration problems

Behavioral Signs and Symptoms

- Insomnia

- Oversleeping

- Relationship problems

- Frequent crying

- Eating more or less than usual

- Cravings

- Sudden anger outbursts

- Substance abuse to relax

- Procrastination and laziness

- Neglecting responsibilities

- Nervous habits such as shaking one's leg or nail-biting

- Withdrawal from society

Physical Signs and Symptoms

- Nausea or dizziness

- Loss of sex drive

- Increased heart rate

- Chest pains

- Aches and pains

- Nervous twitches

- Stomach upset

- Various diseases

- Fainting

- Frequent flu and/or colds

- Constipation or Diarrhea

Anger Management

Anger describes an unpleasant emotion characterized by strong feelings of antagonism and displeasure that ranges from mild irritability or annoyance to intense fury or rage. Our triggers for anger differ from person to person, however, we are exposed to these triggers often. Anger is a normal human emotion that when recognized and appropriate action is taken to deal with it can bear positive outcomes. In this case, it may even become a motivator inspiring one to advocate for social change or stand up for certain injustices. Anger notifies us when we need to take action and rectify something while giving us the motivation, strength, and energy to act. However, when anger is unresolved or left unchecked it can lead to inappropriate and/or aggressive behavior. In this case, it may be referred to as a 'negative' emotion.

Over the past few years especially in the industrial and the now post-industrial era, there has been a significant and continuous rise in stress and anger. This shows that stress has a role in influencing anger. If one is more prone to anger then a lot of stress is likely to trigger feelings of anger. When stress becomes too much and ceases to be a motivator, it may cause us to feel irritable or just angry to the core. When this happens, one is usually overwhelmed with tons of stressors and typically one feels like they lack the resources to deal with stress effectively and has an outburst of anger. This type of stress is referred to as distress. If stressors are understood and steps are taken to maintain equilibrium and deal with the stress, then one can limit distress thereby controlling and limiting one's anger.

Techniques for Anger Relaxation and Management

Techniques for anger relaxation are frequently used in anger management therapy to help us understand our anger and act in ways that are positive to alleviate the negative aspects of anger rather than suppress feelings of anger. These techniques work most effectively when practiced frequently. Some of the techniques are as follows:

Controlled Deep Breathing

When we get angry, several subtle physical changes occur and notify us of these feelings. One of the most noticeable is the change in breathing. When one is angry or upset, their breathing becomes shallow and quick. Noticing this is one of the first steps of this technique. Once one noticed the change in breath, one can make a deliberate effort to deepen and slow their breathing –this will help in maintaining control. These breaths ought to come from your belly rather than your chest. The breaths should be twice as long when coming out as when coming in, for instance, one may breathe in slowly as they count to four and breathe out even slower as they count to eight.

This slow, deep, and deliberate breathing will help relax your breath and return into a normal, relaxed state. Since all things present in the body are interconnected, controlling, and relaxing one's breath should in turn control and relax muscle tensions that are caused by anger thereby reducing feelings of anger significantly.

Progressive Muscle Relaxation

One of the other noticeable physical changes related to anger is muscle tension. This tension can manifest in different parts of one's body and can collectively clump in specific areas such as the neck and shoulders. This tension can even remain long after the anger is gone. Progressive muscle relaxation involves deliberately tensing and tightening your muscles both stressed and unstressed for a slow count of ten then relaxing or releasing these tightened muscles. When practicing this, be sure to release muscles immediately you feel pain. This technique requires you to work progressively from one muscle group to another (for example from head to toe) until you have taken each muscle through a cycle of tension and release. With diligent practice, one may notice their ability to do this cycle of the full body in a few minutes. This technique of tightening and releasing muscles can prove more relaxing than relaxation itself.

Visualizing Yourself to Calmness

Visualization refers to the mental formation or representation of an object, image, situation or set of information. Visualization techniques can also be employed to help with the management of anger. Our brains constantly visualize in the process of simulating future scenarios. This visualization happens so effortlessly that we barely notice it in the same way we barely notice our breathing. When we become aware of our visualization, we can use it as a tool to reduce or reverse anger. Visualization to help with anger is done by imagining a place or scenario that makes you feel calm or relaxed and focusing on details (sometimes with the aid of audio material such as music) such as smells, sounds and how good it feels to be in that space. This is usually done when one is sited comfortably and quietly with their eyes closed.

Visualization has four key benefits that improve how we deal with anger. Firstly, it rewires and programs one's brain to help them realize the strategies, tools, and resources they can use to achieve peace and harmony away from anger. Secondly, it builds our intrinsic motivation to take actions necessary to change the habit pattern of the mind, which is reacting to anger. Thirdly, it sparks one's creative subconscious, which helps us with the sublimation of these negative feelings into more socially acceptable forms of expression such as dance, poetry, music among others. This sublimation helps us express rather than suppress these feelings of anger. Lastly, visualization aids in the law of attraction thereby drawing you closer to circumstances, resources, tools, and people who can help you achieve your goals of anger management.

Various meditation techniques are also used in anger management and relaxation. Mindfulness meditation and Vipassana meditation both encourage us to accept the anger when it manifests itself and observe it as it is without reacting to it or engaging with it. This usually causes us to be fueled and consumed by it causing it to become problematic. In retrospect, when we just simply observe anger as an emotion, neither good nor bad, we learn to work with anger, as it is however or whenever it arises skillfully without it spiraling out of control. When we engage in guided meditation we learn how to relax and gain relief from stress and stressors that may end up causing anger and allow us to process these feelings healthily. This technique can be used with children too especially those with heavy temper tantrums. Peaceful and guided meditations help children, adults, and teens improve self-esteem, relieve anxiety, and stress, and feel generally refreshed in mind, body, and spirit and develop positive mental attitudes in their daily activities.

Grief Management

Grief can be defined as the heightened sense or feeling of pain we feel when we experience loss. This pain is severe as the loss is a reflection of something or someone we love and one may feel engulfed and overwhelmed by it. Grief can follow the loss of someone such as the death of a loved one or the destruction of a relationship to the loss of a pet or even something like the loss of your home. Grief is complex and has no specific rules or set timing. Grief can have symptoms similar to depression such as insomnia, sadness, and loss of interest in self-care. Grief is different from depression as it doesn't impair self-worth. However, grief is not experienced by everyone in the same way. In some cases, it may be accompanied by feelings of guilt or confusion. Prolonged grief can last up to months if not dealt with and can result in isolation as well as chronic loneliness. Nevertheless, its symptoms tend to lessen over time but can be triggered by anniversaries or thoughts about the loss at whatever time.

It has been proposed by professionals in psychology that grief has five stages. These are denial, anger, bargaining, depression, and acceptance. Denial is the first stage of grief and is characterized by the world feeling overwhelming and meaningless. We tend to feel numb and as though life makes absolutely no sense and we wonder how we can go on. In the case of the loss of a loved one, for instance, one may be thinking they cannot live without the deceased and wondering what the point to life without them is. The next stage of grief, which is essential for the healing process, is anger. In the same case, one may be asking questions like "Why did they have to die so soon?" or "Where is God in all of this?"

As one progresses on the path of grief, they get to the next stage of bargaining where one feels like they would do and sacrifice anything and everything for their loved one to be spared their demise. In this case one may begin praying and making promissory offerings to their particular God or Goddess saying things like "I promise to be a better child to my parent if you bring them back," or "I promise to do better for the community if I wake up from this and it's just a dream." During this stage, one is engulfed in 'what-ifs' and 'if only's'. After bargaining, we tend to go deeper into the grief as we bring our attention to the present and face the feelings of emptiness and sadness caused by our loss. This stage usually and feels everlasting, however, it is important to understand that it is an appropriate response to great loss and it will not last forever. This is not a clinical depression or a sign of mental illness.

The last stage of acceptance is usually mixed up with the idea that we should be okay with the loss. However, in reality, most people are never okay with the loss they experience. We usually just learn how to live with it accepting the reality as it is and not as we would like it to be. We accept the new reality as the permanent reality and making it the norm, which we have to adjust to and learn to live with.

Without a doubt, grief is related to and can cause or be caused by stress. Change is one of the reasons stress and grief are intertwined when you lose something, you have to reboot and rearrange things about your life that were connected to the loss, which can potentially act as a stressor. Another reason for this relationship is the pressure from yourself and sometimes society to get over your loss, move on and become 'normal' again. Interpersonal stressors such as hurt feelings, conflict and feelings of alienation and isolation from family and friends following the loss of someone can also be related to this relationship between grief and stress. Internal conflict and an overload of emotions which one usually feel unequipped to handle is another reason for this relationship. Lastly, frustrations that come from not getting what you want are another connecting factor to this relationship. When one experiences grief and loss, they tend to want back what they have lost or wanted a change in circumstances, but our wishes are not what we have in reality causing frustration and stress.

How to Meditate for Grief and Loss

Meditation for grief is one of the most effective ways to deal with grief and loss by helping us get rid of the symptoms of depression and anxiety, pain as well as mend our relationships with others and bring us closure through introspection and reorientation. Breathing meditation and relaxing meditation techniques are good to restore a state of calmness in the mind and body as well as help alleviate certain pains. Guided meditations help us reduce the suffering that comes together with grief. According to teachers of these guided meditations such as Shinzen Young, suffering is a result of pain and resistance. With this understanding, one realizes that they should not resist the loss that has already happened and that they should accept it as part of the experiences in their lives. In as much as pain could be harder to eradicate as it is the mark and relic of love, this understanding reduces suffering significantly and gives us a boost to work patiently and mindfully with ourselves as we reengage with life after whatever loss you have gone through. Mindfulness meditations as well as Vipassana meditation work in this same manner aiming to eradicate the suffering that is accompanied by grief.

Stress and Workplace Awareness Meditation

When working somewhere, one is usually in a different environment with people from all walks of life and pressures from authority figures and oneself. These objects and situations can potentially be acute stressors and trigger; therefore, the stress in the workplace is normal. However, when stress becomes extreme and overwhelming, it can interfere with your productivity, relationships with colleagues, performance, mental and physical health and also spill out to other aspects of your life such as your relationships with friends and family.

While one cannot control the entire workplace environment, there is no need to feel defeated when faced with a difficult situation that triggers stress. When faced with stressors, some steps can be taken to improve your coping skills, relationships in and out of work, productivity, job satisfaction and overall well-being no matter what your individual goals, work demands, and ambitions may be.

Meditation is among the best practices to come out of stressful situations especially at work almost immediately. It works by helping us to regulate our emotions and retuning the brain to be more resilient to stressors. Practicing meditation in the workplace increases our productivity and motivation by turning stress into success. Most people may think of meditation as another task on their to-do list with the demands of a quiet and calm place; however, it is important to understand and take meditation as being able to be in the midst of trouble, noise, and hard work while maintaining calmness and equanimity in your heart. The two most recommended forms of meditation to manage stress in the workplace are transcendental meditation and mindfulness meditation.

Transcendental meditation has a great deal of research backing its ability to help relieve stress at the workplace and reduce cortisol and anxiety. Continuous and diligent practice of transcendental meditation shows to notably improve productivity and work satisfaction so much that business owners and large companies such as General Motors, Sony, Toyota, and

IBM are beginning to invest in meditation programs and making them available for their employees to double their output and wellbeing. This form of meditation shows to improve emotional intelligence, which in turn advances the relationships you have with your colleagues and helps you effectively deal with and express your own emotions.

Mindfulness meditation as a way to deal with workplace stress is more commonly practiced due to the rise in popularity of the practice over the last few years. This technique aims to improve our clarity in our worldly perceptions, which consequently helps us make better decisions. Moreover, being less agitated results in greater inner strength and more stable emotions leading us to be happier and have more fulfilling lives. To reap these benefits, it is important to start meditating especially at the beginning of your day or before you begin working. This can be even easier if you start a meditation group at work with some colleagues and practice mindfulness meditation together before you begin working. It is important to also practice mindful breathing where you randomly take 3-5 mindful breaths and go back to doing what you were doing.

In addition to this, it is also essential to take advantage of the time you use walking as an opportunity to meditate and practice mindful walking. Here one observes their walking with deep awareness and if not in a hurry, it would not hurt to slow down and let your mind follow. Another essential practice tied to mindfulness meditation in the workplace is deep listening. In this case, one listens wholesomely with the intent of understanding as opposed to replying. Normally when we listen with the intent to reply we are usually thinking about our next statement and how to interject our particular opinion rather than taking time to pay attention to and understand fully what the other party has to say. This practice will improve workplace relationships and reduce the frictions and arguments that cause stress at work. Lastly, the practice of mindful speech will also help reduce stress by improving our overall interactions and relationships. When speaking mindfully, one takes the time to think about what they are about to say and visualize and understand the impact it will have on the recipient of the message whether positive or negative. In this case, it is important to consider how our statements will be interpreted and try our best to convey information that will elicit positive consequences and responses.

Abdominal Breathing for Impulse Control

Occasional impulsive behavior is a normal part of life. We experience and engage in impulsivity from time to time whether it is by eating a slice of pizza when on a diet or buying something we do not need. For a person without impulse control however, it is difficult to resist sudden urges, which more often than not seem forceful. For such individuals, it seems like activities that would be deemed normal if done less frequently or less intensely are out of their control. Many are the occasions that these impulsive behaviors violate other people's rights and cause conflict with whatever societal values and norms put in place by one's culture or society. These impulses tend to occur frequently and rapidly without the consideration of the consequences it may breed.

A problem with impulse control is usually noted by a constant repetition of the behavior despite negative consequences, experiencing strong cravings and urges to engage in the problematic behavior, incapability to have power over problem behaviors and engaging in problem behavior to feel pleasure or relieve pressure. Some other symptoms of impulse control are obsessive thoughts, inability to delay instant gratification, lack of patience and severe tension and/or anxiety experienced before engaging in the impulsive behavior. Impulse control can be a key feature or symptom in some mental illnesses such as bulimia and paraphilia; however, some types of impulse control disorders stand as disorders by themselves. Some of the most common forms of impulse control disorders are:

- **Pyromania** – this is the inability to control the urge to set fires. A person with pyromania usually reports feelings for pleasure following their behavior or relief from anxiety or emotional blockage.

- **Kleptomania** – this refers to the uncontrollable urge to steal something and is different from stealing for a necessity such as water or food. In this case, people steal things that are meaningless and unnecessary.

- **Trichotillomania** – This is a disorder that is usually characterized by a strong urge to pull out one's hair. Even when this act is painful, the urge surpasses any concern for pain.

- **Intermittent explosive disorder** – this refers to the inability to control anger outbursts to even the smallest of triggers whereby the rage can spill out of control and turn into physical acts of violence.

- **Pathological gambling** – also referred to as compulsive gambling it was once considered an impulse control disorder but recent research shows that it is more of a process addiction. Here one is unable to resist the urge to gamble. The thought of gambling becomes too overpowering causing one to feel like engaging in gambling is the only relief they can get.

- **Unspecified impulse-control disorder** – in this case, one shows the general signs and symptoms of an impulse-control disorder however, the impulse observed does not fall into any pre-recognized criteria.

One of the most recommended techniques to control one's impulses is abdominal breathing. This technique is similar to mindful breathing in that one deliberately slows down and deepens their breath. When practicing this, you need to inhale slowly through your nose then exhale even slower through your mouth while making a hissing sound almost like a balloon losing air trying to make the hiss last as long as possible. This technique involves controlling your breath to calm you down and reduce your cravings and urges.

Chapter 5: Meditation for Anxiety

Throughout this book, we have taken the time to understand anxiety, its triggers, signs, and some of the types of anxiety disorders. It has become clear that everyone faces anxiety at one point in their lives while others seem to have it constantly haunting them. It also became clear how the word does not get the recognition it deserves.

In this chapter, we are going to look into different meditation techniques which are used to deal with anxiety and panic disorders. If you are suffering from either, this is the book for you. Who knows, it might save you the frequent trips to the doctor to get anxiety pills. Systematically, this chapter guides the reader through the various techniques known to deal with both anxiety and panic attacks.

Anxiety and Stress Relief

The goal of anxiety and stress relief meditation is to learn how to let go of whatever is weighing you down and realize the peace and calmness the mind can experience. It serves the purpose of helping someone understand the position they are now in. The past and the future are impermanent. By letting these thoughts cloud our judgment and state of mind, we accept the troubles they drag along with them.

When it comes to anxiety and stress relief, it is highly advisable to separate yourself from everyone else. You need time to restore yourself to your most productive element because you might rub off some of the bad energy onto others. If need be, hide in a properly ventilated closet-as long as you are comfortable.

Close your eyes and try to relax your body. This is important to prepare it to get into a state of well-being. Focus your attention on yourself. This is your time; forget all the other things that cloud your mind. You want to be at peace and resonate peace and this is your time to manifest its existence. Start by inhaling and exhaling slowly through the nose and mouth in that order. Observe your body and the buildup of tension accumulated from the anxiety and stress.

You can imagine a stream of river passing and washing away all the buildup of anxiety and stress. Let it all go; let it all wash away. You can imagine anything. You can also decide to fold your stress and anxiety in a leaf and let it go in whichever direction the wind decides. Every time you exhale, envision all the worries go away. Your mind is your palace of imagination. You can do anything in the space you have created for yourself now.

Slowly, go back and observe your breathing again. Keep inhaling through your nose and exhaling through the mouth. You can decide to let it happen naturally or give it intervals of three seconds. Your space your choice. If your mind keeps wandering, you can perform a couple of deep breaths to bring back your focus to your breathing.

Now, imagine you are all alone at the beach and you have worn your favorite pair of swimsuits. You want to take a dip because you are aware of the calming effect water has on you. Picture yourself running towards the water and splashing your way in. To your surprise, when you take a dip, you start to glow and feel so nice. The more you dip yourself into the water, the more your worries wash away leaving you with a nice aura and a sense of peace. Keep imagining this before going back to observe your breathing.

Notice if there is any change in your breathing. Does it feel more natural and relaxed? Do you feel better? If not, start with the breathing again. Center yourself and your thoughts. Do not let your source of stress or anxiety plague you in this space. Remember, this is your personal space. This is your time. Nobody can take away your time.

You can use any relevant scenario as a visual tool to let go of the stress and anxiety that had manifested itself. It does not have to be exactly what is above. If it works for you, that is all that matters. Keep transitioning from your breathing to visual scenarios until the time you desire. Even after feeling better, you might decide to continue doing it for a while just because you can. There is certainly no harm in that.

Apart from the above method, mindfulness meditation, some audio guided meditations and Vipassana meditation serve as good alternatives to try. The practice of meditation does not restrict you from trying out something different if the one you are accustomed to doing does not show results. Any technique that is good for you is the best.

Self-Healing for On-The-Spot Anxiety

Anxiety can clock in at any time it feels like. Let us compare it to that manager who decides to walk into the office, yet nobody expected them to show up because it was their day off. From minor misunderstandings to large problems, anxiety always comes packed differently to every individual. Luckily, several methods that deal with anxiety immediately occur exist. These methods are:

Mindful Breathing

Take some time out for yourself for just five minutes. If you cannot, just pay attention to yourself wherever you are and start to breathe deeply while assuming an upright posture. Notice how the lower section of your bells expands as you breathe in through your nose and contracts as you breathe out through your mouth. Deep breathing is associated with lowering the heart rate, which in turn reduced blood pressure.

Focus on the Present

As soon as you feel the anxiety starting to kick in, in whatever situation you are, just start to focus on what is happening presently. If you are walking, focus on how your feet hit the ground and how the wind is blowing against your face or hair. If you are eating, focus on how your fingers feel holding that spoon. What kind of sensations do you feel around your mouth as you eat? Pay attention to these details and slowly witness yourself starting to feel less tense.

Scan Your Body

This technique combines bodily awareness and breathing. It helps individuals experience the connection between the body and the mind. Start by observing your breathing. Inhale and exhale through your nose. The purpose is to clear all the stories in your head and concentrate on yourself. After a few minutes, focus your attention on a specific group of muscles and release any tension you feel. Move to the next muscle and so the same. Keep doing this until you have covered the whole body. You can do it in whatever order you like.

Use Guided Imagery

Due to the availability of the internet, it is easy to find apps or audios online that can help you create guided images. However, this technique might not be so efficient for people who have a problem constructing mental images. If you have the ability to construct mental images with ease, make sure that the imageries are relatable to you. Otherwise, you might not understand what is going on-which beats the whole point. Guided imageries are there to help someone reinstate the positivity in themselves. If you find it difficult to visualize such images in your mind, you can stare at one imagine for a few seconds, and then close your eyes with the idea of retaining the image in your mind. As you practice this technique, you will find it to be easier and easier to achieve mental imagery.

Start Counting

In school, it was a common thing to hear teachers or parents say, "If you feel angry or you want to say something out of bitterness, just count to ten first." It is funny how this holds true. Counting is one of the many easy ways to deal with your anxiety anywhere it occurs. You do not have to count to ten; you can even do it to one hundred if it feels right. Challenge yourself and count backward as well. This way, you can really get your mind into it.

Sometimes the anxiety goes away quickly, while other times it does not. Whatever the case, ensure you try to keep calm and collected. Counting distracts you from the cause of anxiety and keeps your mind busy. This will eventually return you to a state of calm.

Interrupt Your Thoughts

From my experience with anxiety, your thoughts can so powerful to the extent of making you actually feel like your fears are going to manifest themselves. The thought itself then again doubles your anxiety and the cycle just keeps going. Then again, you realize that the majority of these things never get to happen and that you were so anxious for no good reason.

Interrupting your thoughts as they come can bring you back to a sense of calm. You can do this by starting to think about a person you love- a person who brings peace into your life. If you like a certain music album, skip to your favorite songs and jam along. Remember to always return your focus to yourself and observe how you feel after a few minutes. Observe how none of these feelings is permanent.

With these few tips, you are ready to break your anxiety cycle.

Panic Attacks

A panic attack is an unexpected feeling of intense fear that leads to other serious physical responses where no actual risk or obvious cause is present. They may occur at any time, even when you are asleep. Sometimes they have no trigger. A panic attack gives you breathing difficulties, makes your heart pound and it gives you a feeling that you are going crazy or are about to die. It is not a pretty experience just from what it sounds like. Other symptoms that occur may include sweating, shaking, fever, nausea, your legs may 'turn to jelly' and feeling a disconnection from yourself.

Many people only get to experience less than five panic attacks in their lifetime. The problem usually then goes away after the stressful episode has ended. Some people have very constantly recurring panic attacks and they happen to stay in constant fear with the danger of having another panic attack-these people suffer from a condition called panic disorder.

It is difficult to pinpoint what exactly causes feelings of panic and the onset of attacks, but they tend to be common in families. Major life events such as marriage, graduation and retirement and the death of someone you love also show a bond with panic attacks and panic disorders. Some medical conditions can also be cause panic attacks such as hyperthyroidism and low blood sugar. The use of stimulants in the likes of caffeine and cocaine can also trigger panic attacks and disorders. If you suffer from panic disorders, it would be advisable to refrain from such.

In the event that you have had a panic attack and it has passed, it would be nice to give your body what it needs. You might feel fatigued, hungry, or even thirsty. Make sure you give yourself some good treatment after it happens. It is advisable to inform someone that you can confide in about the situation. It is not a bad thing to ask for help.

Below are breathing techniques that reverse the symptoms of panic disorders.

Diaphragm Meditation for Panic Attacks

When we encounter a situation of distress, the pattern and rate of our breathing become different. On a normal day, we always breathe slowly using our lower lungs. However, in situations of distress, our breathing shifts to be shallow and rapid while situated in the upper lungs. In the event that it happens when resting, it can cause hyperventilation. This also explains some of the symptoms experienced during panic. Luckily, by knowing how to change your breathing, you can start to reverse the symptoms of your panic attack.

The body has a natural calming response called the parasympathetic response that triggers by changing how you breathe. It is very powerful and is the complete opposite of the emergency response (the feelings that kick in during an attack). When the calming response comes into play, all the primary changes brought about by the emergency response start to shift.

The two meditation techniques recommended to help with this disorder are natural breathing technique and the calming counting technique. The natural breathing technique is pretty much the same thing as the abdominal breathing technique. If you can practice breathing like this on a daily basis, it will only prove beneficial.

The Natural Breathing Technique (Abdominal Breathing Method)

Gently inhale a normal amount of air through your nostrils making sure it fills your lower lungs. You can decide to place your hands beneath your lower belly to supervise this or you can do whatever seems comfortable. Make sure to exhale easily while focusing on the movements of your lower belly. Feel it expand as air gets in and go down when you exhale. Carry this practice with a relaxed mindset not forgetting to fill your lower lungs with air. Try your best to actually "feel" the oxygen rushing into your body and making its way through your blood. You will feel how every tissue in your body imbibes the fresh oxygen you have just inhaled.

Calming Counts

Assume a comfortable sitting posture and take a deep breath. As you are exhaling, slowly whisper to yourself to relax. Keep your eyes closed to avoid losing focus. Now, start taking natural breaths while counting down from a desired number. Make sure to only count after a successful exhale. As you keep breathing, throw your attention to any areas of tension. Imagine the tension getting loose and shriveling, leaving you feeling calm and refreshed.

When you arrive at the end of your countdown, open your eyes, and notice any difference in what you are feeling. If it has worked but not as efficiently as desired, give it a longer try making sure your willpower is set to let go of the panic. Eventually, you will notice yourself get better.

Studies have shown that these meditation techniques, if practiced even when one is not anxious, are bound to yield the same results. If you can, dedicate a little time every morning and evening to practice the technique that works best for you.

Two things should be highly observed when practicing these techniques: focusing on changing negative thoughts and not thinking of anything else while meditating. This is because our thoughts directly influence our breathing and changing your negative thoughts can help lessen the symptoms quickly. Concentrate most of your effort into not thinking about anything else. Do not even think about your next breath; it should happen naturally.

Chapter 6: Wading Off Pain
with Meditation

In this chapter, we are going to be taking a look at how meditation can help relieve pain. Since birth, we have all experienced one sort of pain or another. Simply put, pain can be understood as a strong and unpleasant physical sensation that follows illness or injury. There are various types of pain many of which are disease-related and others that are caused by psychological factors and injuries. However, whatever type of pain you experience, it is possible to categorize it between acute pain, which can last for a moment, and chronic pain, which usually persists for long periods.

People who experience a lot of chronic pain usually can trace their pain to a particular stressor, which causes anxiety. This relationship brings the chicken-egg question: does pain cause anxiety or does anxiety cause pain? When understood and observed keenly, one sees that it is a two-way traffic −pain can cause anxiety and anxiety can also bring about pain. Some chronic pain disorders such as fibromyalgia, migraines, lower back pains, and irritable bowel syndrome cause an overlap of anxiety, pain, and depression. Many individuals suffering from such diseases have anxiety as well. This could be because chronic pain is discomforting and depressing. Research has also shown that the brain and nervous systems work with parts of the body and that pain, anxiety, and depression share some biological and psychological mechanisms. Anxiety, especially when chronic, can be the cause of some pains and tensions such as body soreness, headaches, and muscle tension.

Pain Relief Management

Relaxation, which may seem like a simple concept, can sometimes be hard to achieve, especially with individuals who suffer from chronic pain. Relaxation involves being able to take your mind off things such as the pain you are experiencing or the trigger causing anxious feelings and stress. Relaxing taking your mind off the pain can significantly reduce pain levels in the body and reap mental and physical benefits even when done for a few minutes. Relaxation can be anything from breathing exercises and meditation to painting or gardening. Whatever method one chooses to employ in the attempt of relaxation should reduce stress by helping you ease built-up tensions in the body and reduce pain, thereby improving overall body wellbeing.

Lately, some pain relaxation techniques such as guided imagery, relaxation, breathing techniques, progressive muscle relaxation, music, massages, and stretches can help with labor pains by giving the brain a source of positive distraction. This, in turn, stimulates the release of endorphins in the body, rewiring your brain to think of the pains as productive, manageable, and positive.

Meditation Techniques That Reduce Pain

Some of the meditation techniques used for pain relaxation are:

Guided Imagery

This technique is similar to the visualization technique we covered in the anger management. Breathing deeply and slowly, one is to imagine a peaceful and tranquil scene in which one feels relaxed, calm, safe and comfortable. When doing this pay attention to the smallest details such as the smells, colors and sounds surrounding the visualized area.

Breathing Meditation

This like mindful breathing involves taking slow, deep, deliberate breaths to achieve relaxation by calming the mind.

Self-Talk

This like transcendental meditation involves repeating a mantra, quote or positive affirmation about oneself and the pain they are experiencing. For instance, instead of paying attention to the fact that one may not be able to finish their tasks in time due to some certain pain one can relax and remind themselves continuously that "no harm will come to anyone if I don't finish my task on time but I can get a lot done by taking it slow.

Vipassana Meditation

Sit in a quiet place and observe your breathing while maintaining an equal state of mind (without trying to control it and just simply being aware). Whenever thoughts and pain arise, simply be aware of them and notice them without wishing for another experience or trying to push the experience away. Think of this experience as a passing cloud understanding that everything is impermanent. This technique is similar to mindfulness meditation, which uses just about the same instructions in an aim to relax and calm your mind causing pain and tension relief.

Chapter 7: Getting Some Sleep

In this chapter, we will take look at how people suffering from insomnia can use meditation to achieve sleep. You may be surprised to be one of the lucky people who get actually get a great deal of sleep as compared to others. Approximately 25% of Americans suffer from insomnia, but according to the most recent research, only about 75% of them recover without feeling the effects of bad sleep patterns or chronic insomnia. Worldwide studies indicate that one in every five people is suffering from insomnia as well.

Insomnia is easily the world's most common sleeping disorder. Insomnia is the inability to stay or fall asleep even when presented with the opportunity to do so. Victims are prone to experience fatigue, concentration difficulties, decreased output, and mood swings.

The type of insomnia one has is distinguishable from the duration it lasts. Acute insomnia occurs for a very short duration, such as when it is caused by everyday circumstances of life. For example, when you are about to go for a big trip and you are full of excitement, you might have some difficulty sleeping. The same goes for other major situations that crop up with everyday life. Eventually, this sleep disruption meets exhaustion and resolves itself without treatment.

On the other hand, chronic insomnia is sleep disruption that occurs three nights every week for up to a three-month duration. Respiratory conditions such as sleep apnea and asthma, pain, anxiety, depression, menopause, urinary incontinence, and acid reflux are some of the underlying causes of chronic insomnia. Some medications and lifestyle patterns may also step in the way of your sleep, driving you to chronic insomnia. Insomniacs do sleep but the quality of the sleep they get is so low.

In store for you in this chapter are different meditation practices that can help you achieve your desired sleep cycle.

Types of Meditations to Practice for Insomnia

Are you tired of staring at the ceiling or watching your watch clock by as you wait to sleep? Insomnia is one of the most annoying uninvited guests. It may develop the habit of overstaying, leaving you to be its prisoner for an unspecified period. However, if you are tired of gazing at the ceiling every night and want to do something about it, here are a couple of meditation techniques that prove to beat insomnia:

Talking to Oneself

Holding a conversation with yourself is probably one of the most underrated methods one can use to fall asleep. Most people associate talking to themselves to being given names like 'crazy' or 'geek' but this simple practice can change your sleep patterns for the better.

Insomniacs are good at hurling negative things their own way. Some get to the point of harming themselves because they are so angry with themselves for not being able to sleep. Paradoxically, insomnia tends to feed on the criticism one gives to self. Not everyone gets to the point of inflicting physical harm to himself or herself. Sometimes, the brain fills with negative chatter and questions that only harm sleep progress.

Offer yourself calming words of appreciation and understanding during this time as you talk to yourself. Apply words like "I am sure I can do this" or "It may take some time, but it will work out eventually" or "Everything will be better with persistence." The aim of these positive statements is to reduce any negative feelings and those of anxiety in order to achieve sleep. Negative thoughts will only be a cause for more stress which later builds up to anxiety or even panic attacks.

Mindful Body Scan

This type of meditation is very easy to perform. Conveniently, it can happen as you lie in bed. Rumor has it that it is one of the most popular techniques used by people from the military to achieve sleep.

A body scan involves paying attention to different parts of your body and releasing the tension that has accumulated. A top to bottom approach (or vice versa) usually characterizes it where you can choose to either start from the tip of your head or your feet. The goal is to work your way to the opposite end while releasing tension from each muscle. The duration to do this can vary depending on the severity of the insomnia. Whatever happens, focus on your muscles, and keep releasing the tension.

Use of Mantras

Developing a mantra can act as a good tool to achieve mental clarity while setting your attention on a given phrase. While addressing the issue of mantras, many people form an associative link with yoga and meditation. Actually, they are usable in many more scenarios besides the mentioned ones. The aim of using mantras is to ensure your mind has no room for other thoughts since insomniacs have a tendency of constantly battling fleeting memories.

Even on the occasion that you do not fall asleep, you will be able to notice your mind will be quieter. This means your mind will eventually end up resting some of its regions giving it a little physical rest. If you are lying comfortably, this will restore your body to some extent.

Although most of the original mantras appeared in Sanskrit, they come in different forms. To keep yourself concentrated, always choose a simple mantra. The following guidelines can help you come up with a good one:

- It should be clear with simple wording.

- It should be very short to avoid you from thinking about the process.

- It should have a calming effect.

- It should have an affirmative tone.

When reciting a mantra, your only concern should be saying it internally as you lie down in a comfortable position. Avoid any positions that will lead to twiddling, as this will only reverse your efforts. Try to lie still and breathe deeply as you recite it. Again, if your mind starts racing, refocus your attention back to the mantra.

Visualization

Instead of spending most of your time thinking about your stressful day or your next exam or meeting, try visualization. It can be a good practice to help you unwind and fall asleep easily by focusing their attention on calming and soothing images.

Imagine yourself in a place where you experienced a deep sense of calm. Feel free to make your imagination wild. Imagine yourself on your way to that place again and it will be a better experience than you had the previous time. Making your imagination as detailed as possible should be one of your prime goals. What time is it? What kind of clothes are you wearing? What can you see along the way? Keep at it until you sleep.

This method can also be very useful when one decides to use guided meditation. Most scripts require you to imagine a calming scene and if you are good at it, you are halfway there.

Counting Backwards

Counting forward is so easy. You can probably do it while asleep. If counting from 100 seems a bit difficult for you, you can always start from 50 or 70. Make sure you restart when your mind drifts and you lose track. Do not take it too seriously that you beat yourself up when you lose count. This is just a casual exercise. Nobody is watching.

Sleep Hypnosis Script

It is a good idea to familiarize yourself with sleep hypnosis techniques, considering how important sleep is for our daily functioning. A healthy mind is a wealthy mind. Without a proper good night's sleep, you are bound to run out of energy. Since 50% of the world suffers from insomnia, I would like to share two sleep hypnosis scripts that might come in handy. You can record them in your own voice for personal use when going to sleep.

Script 1

Lie flat on your back and feel the sensations on your body for a while. Spread your hands and feet comfortably to make sure you are fully relaxed. Now I want you to focus your attention on your breath. I want you to breathe in deeply and fill the bottom of your lungs, causing the lower belly to rise. Hold your breath for a few seconds and slowly release the air while feeling your lower belly drop. Make sure you have emptied every drop of air from your lungs.

Start again by noticing how fresh the air is as you breathe in. Pay attention to filling your lower lungs with air as you feel your stomach rise again. Make sure you have fully filled your lungs with air that you cannot take in more. Pause for a few seconds and let go of the air slowly. Repeat this process seven times. Each time, imagine your body relaxing and letting go of all the tension you have. Let it all fade away as sand washed off by water.

Now, try to feel every bit of your body. Notice any points of tension and just make a note of them. I want you to start relaxing your muscles from the top of your head to your toes.

Tense the crown of your head and release the tension, pushing it to the left side of the head. Tense the left side of your head and release any tension left while pushing it to the right side of the head. Do the same for the right side of the head and push the tension to the back of the head. Now, bring your attention to your forehead. Tense your forehead and do away with any tense sensation. If there are still traces of tension, move to the left and right eyebrow. Each time, make sure you tense each part and release the tension, pushing whatever residual tension left to the next part of the body. Do this twice since is a key area of stress. From your eyebrows, drop down to your nose and tense it making sure to release the tension after a few seconds. Now go to the jaw region and do the same.

Imagine all your tension accumulated at the jaw. Move it down to your neck through your throat. This time too, tense your neck and release the tension twice. When done, you are free to move to your chest region.

From the chest region, repeat the same process, covering each part systematically and not neglecting any region. When you encounter an area with a lot of tension, tense it and release it twice then progress to the other part.

After completing the cycle of the chest and stomach region, transfer your attention to your upper back. Feel any tension present on your left scapula. Your scapula is the bone that is present on the upper back. Tense it and release the tension after a few seconds. Transfer the tension to the right scapula and tense it as well. Release the tension each time making sure to transfer the tension left to the next part of the body. Now continue with the process until you reach your lower back. Make sure to release all the tension or carry the residual to the next part. Now, bring all your tension to the tip of your spine, close to the neck, and imagine it sliding down to join both scapulae and connecting to the shoulders.

Focus on the fingers from the left hand now. Relax and stretch your hand. Tense the muscles in your hand and transfer to your wrist any remaining tension. Add tension then relax, transferring to your forearm the remaining tension. Add tension then relax, and then transfer to your upper arm any remaining tension. Tense, relax, and shift to your shoulder any remaining tension. Repeat the same process for the right hand. When you bring the final tension to your left shoulder, slide both accumulated tensions down to the spine and through the scapulae to the hips.

Tense the hips and relax. Imagine the tension left whirling around in a circle just disbanding itself disappearing. Tense the hips and relax them again. Now, move any tension left in the opposite direction and think of it being washed away by a calming feeling.

Move any residual tension to the thighs. Tense both of them simultaneously and relax. Carry any residual tension to the knees. Tense both of them and relax. Make sure to keep conscious of the moving tension to ensure the previous areas are free of tension. Move down to the shins, tensing them and relaxing them simultaneously after a few seconds. Carry any residual tension to the calves. Tense them and relax them twice. This is a big area of tension. Pay close attention to it as you transfer any residual tension to the ankles. Tense and relax the ankles twice as well. Move to the heels and do the same. Tense and relax them foot by foot. Release all the tension and transfer any left tension to the toes. Imagine all the tension oozing out from the tips of your toes and flowing out of your body. You now feel relaxed and ready to encounter the next journey to sleep.

Now with your completely relaxed body laying still on the bed, feel your body getting lighter and lighter. You can envision yourself floating up and heading for the clouds. You want to go and lay on the cushions of the clouds. Your body, mind, and spirit is calm. You are now in the midst of heavy cushiony clouds. You can feel them comfortably rubbing on your skin as you drift into more cloud comfort. They just keep coming and ones that are more comfortable keep showing up. You can also feel a slight gentle breeze drift you away. You are relaxed.

Now imagine yourself lying still in a drifting boat that keeps rowing from side to side in a slow-moving river. The clouds are still your cushion and it is the most comfortable thing you have ever experienced. You are not worried where the river is flowing to; you are just drifting off with it, letting the rowing and the comfort of the cloud blanket be the center of your attention. You are in a safe environment. Anywhere you go is a familiar place. You can always find your way back home.

Look at the sides of the boat. Look how beautiful the trees are on each side, leaning a bit closer to the river. Notice how they form a protective canopy around you, protecting you from the sun and strong winds. It is cool and calm. Just the right thing for you.

The birds are chirping with lulling songs. You like the song. You like the place. There are rays of sunshine peering through cracks from the canopy giving you a warm feeling. The boat is still rowing. The comfort of the clouds still engulfs you. There is no concept of time in this space as well. Time is completely still. Your only concern is the relaxed feeling that has taken over your body. You can feel the sounds of the river flowing; it is so gentle and peaceful yet confident. This makes you feel stress-free and calm. You do not have any care in the world.

Take two last deep breaths. The purpose is to put your body into deeper relaxation as you prepare to drift into deep sleep. Feel yourself sink further into your bed as you drift off into deep sleep. You are at peace and safe.

Script 2

This guided sleep meditation will help you relax and dive into a peaceful and restful slumber.

Begin in a comfortable position. Lie on your back with your hands at your sides or in your thighs. You have permission to switch positions at any moment to ensure maximum comfort but for now, begin by lying comfortably on your back.

Do a quick mental scan on your body for any areas with tension. Take this time note, fully, how your body feels. In this session, your focus will be releasing all types of tension in your body and silencing the mind. As soon as your mind is blank and free from anger and anxiety, you will easily find yourself engulfed by peaceful sleep.

Imagine that the air around you is full of life and healing and breathe in

Exhale slowly, expelling any tension.

You might be thinking about what you accomplished today and what you will need to accomplish tomorrow.

Maybe you are worried about a certain situation or individual. Perhaps you are concerned about the circumstances which are surrounding you at any given moment. Ideally, you would be able to identify what is affecting you.

In order to achieve relaxation and eventually sleep, you should now erase everything from your mind so that tomorrow you will be relaxed, alert, and able to handle your responsibilities with a positive mentality.

Take some time to ponder on what you usually do before you sleep. For the next few minutes, do any fretting or pondering you decide on. You should now erase everything from your mind. Your focus should not be on anything else at this moment other than clearing your mind. You should not be pondering anything other than soothing, unclenched thoughts

Take this moment to take into full account how your body feels.

Where is all the pent-up tension stored today? Focus all your energy on the area of your body that is experiencing the most tension. Focus all your energy on the smallest point of tension. Take a deep breath in and surround the tension, and as you exhale that breath, release all the tension with a sigh of relief.

Pay attention to the area in your body that is the most relaxed. Feel the relaxation build up with every breath you take. Let the feeling of relaxation explore your body further and further.

As you feel the sleep oozing into your system, feel your mind go deeper and deeper into the calm sensation. For the following minutes, you may decide to focus on counting down as you breathe, and become more and more relaxed with each breath you take or as you continue counting. Focus your energy and attention on the number one and breathe calmly.

As you breathe, take your time to count from one, slowly getting to ten as you become calmer and your body more relaxed. As you let go, you need to allow yourself to drown in your relaxation and drift into a deep, refreshing slumber.

Continue breathing and mindfully count with me.

One, continue focusing on the number one as you breathe.

Two, you can feel yourself progressively sink into relaxation. The deeper you go, the calmer you get. Wallow in the peace.

Three, allow all the tension and negativity to escape your body. Let rest and relaxation fill your entire being. Concentrate on your breathing and the numbers.

Picture the number four as you sink deeper into relaxation. You can feel the relaxation move throughout your body, from your feet all the way to your arms. You feel your body becomes heavier and heavier due to relaxation.

Focus all your remaining energy on the number five. Allow your body and mind to sink deeper and deeper. Accept sleep's warm embrace.

Six, you are experiencing intense relaxation.

Seven, accept the calmness that is embracing your body and mind.

Eight, peaceful and intense relaxation.

Nine, now allow your mind to sink deeper with a lack of direction. Explore the intense relaxation and embrace it.

Ten, relaxation is flowing everywhere.

Now, you may do this again, but this time start with ten and slowly flow to one. When you get to one, you will experience total and complete relaxation and sink into a heavy slumber. When I instruct you to commence, countdown slowly as my voice plays in the background.

Your focus should only be on the numbers as I narrate the experience of relaxation. You may now begin at ten. As you breathe, take your time to move down to nine. Slowly continue the countdown independently.

Sink deeper and deeper into relaxation. Accept the warm embrace of deep sleep. Ensure that you are still comfortable and drifting in peace.

Slumber. Calmness. Peaceful and relaxing. Sinking. Sinking deeper. Embracing and accepting. Relaxation. Sleep. Feeling engulfed by peace. Pleasant peace. Peaceful with yourself. Confident. Caring. Refreshing. Relaxation. Heavy relaxation. Deep sleep. Peaceful and relaxed.

Silence. Soothing sleep. Deep relaxation. Calm and relaxed breathing. Let the warmth and calmness embrace you. Relaxation. Peace. Deeper relaxation. Peaceful sleep. Accepting the warm embrace and sinking into a deep sleep. Deep, peaceful sleep. Sleep.

Creating the Ideal Sleep Environment

Trying to sleep in a setting that is not conducive for you can be quite the task. Unless you're the environment around is set up just right, you may keep tossing and turning in bed until you reach a point of exasperation. Sometimes we set ourselves up for failure by ignoring a couple of conditions that might greatly influence our sleeping patterns. If getting some sleep is among your topmost priorities, making sure that you set up a good environment can leap you to depths of sleep you could never imagine. Here are some things you need to do to switch up your room:

Make the Bed Comfortable

If you have been sleeping on the same mattress with a big depression at the center for the last 20 years, there is a big chance you can barely score any sleep. If you wake up with a stiff back and the feeling of tire yet you seem to enjoy sleeping in other places, you might need to replace that mattress. This goes for the pillows too. If you keep shifting them during the night, it might be time to get a new one.

The thought of the expenditure might be a huge blow to deal with but if it comes between you and getting a good rest, I suggest preferring the latter. We all spend a huge part of our day lying in bed to achieve some sort of relaxation. It is only fair to give ourselves a good experience, as sleep itself is important for our daily functioning. If purchasing a new mattress and pillow seems like a huge amount to cough up now, there are other easy methods applicable online that can be of help.

Keep the Right Temperature

Do you constantly stay up at night because you cannot stop sweating? Do you receive sleep interruptions when you wake up in the middle to change your sweaty clothes? It would be a good idea to observe what level of temperature serves you best before you sleep next time.

Research has it that when your body is preparing itself for slumber, the temperatures drop significantly. Keeping your room cool can provide a conducive environment for you to achieve the level of rest you require. A good tip would be to sleep with no clothes on. Not only does this increase the chance of a good night's sleep, it also works by reducing any temperature build up that the body might experience.

Keep it Quiet

Unwanted sounds are also some of the biggest thieves sleep has ever seen. The source of the disturbance may not matter. The idea that there is a source of disturbance in the first place is the only thing that needs to worry you. Noise of whatever magnitude can do a bad number on your sleep cycle. Watching out on this disturbance and trying to eliminate it can be of great help to achieve sound sleep.

Getting a sound machine can be a good leap to counter this. Sound machines get fame from their smooth lulling sounds that drown all the other surrounding sounds. This can help in creating a soothing environment for someone to sleep. It the thought of sounds, in general, do not sit well with you, getting earplugs can do the trick.

Do Away with Gadgets

Are you still trying to sleep while busy clutching your phone? Wow! I am not judging, but do you know the light emitted from smartphones, tablets, and TV are only responsible for stealing sleep? Furthermore, most of these things are so engaging that you are definitely bound to have trouble while trying to achieve some sleep. Moreover, the owners of these sources of media hire professionals who give them advice on tactics usable to ensure people stay hooked to whatever they are engaging in. Therefore, clutching onto your phone, tablet, or TV while trying to sleep does not really fit the category of 'best ideas ever.'

Placing your digital alarm clock a bit far from your view is also something to look into. Most people suffering from insomnia keep getting a lot of disturbance from the light. To make the torment more for themselves, they keep checking the time and only panic more when they see how much time is fleeting. The best idea would be to face it away from you at a distance from the bed. This way, you will also not get late to wake up because you will always have to stand to put off your alarm.

Clear the Clutter

You really do not need to keep your room stocked up like a gym. Aiming for a clean room with nothing else but your bed and clothes can really improve your sleep. Having so many things in your bedroom other than what you need to sleep will only make your mind associate the room with them. Now your bedroom will not be a place to sleep; it will be a place to study, play games, and hike on the mountain of clothes on the floor.

When you completely associate your room with sleep, your mind will always be in tune with the idea that the room means bedtime. Have you ever heard people say that they always get a good night's sleep after cleaning their room? Well, it just might be true.

Keep It Dark

Artificial light mimics natural light while emitting a blue light that keeps people awake. A good way to achieve sleep would be to keep the room as dark as possible. Having heavy blinds to counter any outside light is highly advised. This also means you need to get rid of light emitters such as glow lamps and night-lights.

If eliminating your cellphone from your room does not seem so reasonable, always keep it screen-side down and on silent. When phones light up with new texts and e-mails, your sleep is bound to be distracted and your attention captured as well. You might end up using the time to get sleep to check on your emails-which is not what we want.

Aromatherapy

Research has shown that it can help to encourage sleep by using certain scents in a room. What aromatherapy does is create a pleasant and calming atmosphere that can assist you to settle down. It's also nice as part of a routine that your brain will pick up as a cue that it's almost time to go to sleep through ongoing use. Lavender and vanilla are some of the recommended scents to use.

Your Room Color

A UK study showed that your bedroom color could have an effect on how much sleep you get. They made a discovery in a study of over 2,000 British households that the colors blue, yellow, and green helped sleepers get the most hours of sleep. Often these colors are associated with calm and relaxation and c an help make your mind feel comfortable as you try to rest.

Colors like violet, brown and gray can possibly destroy the quantity of sleep you get at the other end of the spectrum. Theories indicate that purple is an artistic color that stimulates the creative mind, and often dreariness and depression are linked with brown and grey.

Clearly, so many things can come between you and your forty winks. Coming across this book might have helped you find out some of the things that come between you and a peaceful night. Some of these things may be out of your budget but I bet you can always find a compromise for some of them if not all. The bottom line is, in order to maximize the amount of sleep you get, you need to prioritize your sleep like any other task.

Benefits of Good Sleep

Getting little, or no sleep one night, can really make your mood fluctuate the next day. If the cycle keeps going every night, the lack of sleep will do a number on more than just your moods. Studies indicate that periodic quality sleep can help enhance all kinds of problems, from blood sugar to workouts. A few more reasons come into play:

A Sharper Mind

You will likely have difficulty holding on to and remembering information when you run low on sleep. That is because, in both learning and memory, sleep plays a large role. Without sufficient sleep, focusing and receiving fresh data is hard. There is also not enough time for your brain to store memories correctly so you can pick them up later. With enough sleep, your brain will be able to catch up and prepare you for the next day.

Stress Reduction

When your body does not receive the right sleep time, it can counter the process by releasing stress hormones. The processing of your feelings is another thing your brain does while you sleep. This time your mind requires acknowledging and responding in the correct manner. You tend to have more adverse emotional responses and less favorable ones when you cut that short.

Chronic lack of sleep may also increase the likelihood of a mood disorder. One major research showed you are five times more probable to create depression when you have insomnia, and your chances of anxiety or panic disorders are even higher.

Refreshing sleep enables you to hit a poor day's reset button, enhance your life perspective, and be better ready for difficulties.

Regulate Blood Sugar

The quantity of glucose in your blood falls during the profound, slow-wave portion of your sleep cycle. In this deepest stage, not enough time means you do not get that break to allow a reset- like the volume turned up. Your body will find it more difficult to respond to the requirements of your cells and the concentrations of blood sugar.

By denying yourself the ability to achieve and maintain deep sleep, you run the risk of getting type 2 diabetes, heart attacks, and strokes.

Regulating Your Weight

You are bound to be hungrier if you have not received enough rest. Sleep deprivation interferes with leptin and ghrelin, which are the hormones responsible for appetite control. When these hormones are imbalanced, you are less likely to resist food that is unhealthy for you. Therefore, sleep will not necessarily help you lose weight but it can help regulate the hormones responsible for it.

Furthermore, when you are tired and sleepy, you are less likely to want to take that midnight stroll to the fridge.

A Germ Killer

Research actually proves that plenty of sleep can help the body fight ailments. In the event that you are hurt from an injury, some good sleep will help helps reduce the pain. Studies have linked lower pain threshold and sleep loss to go hand in hand. Your immune system recognizes and destroys harmful bacteria and viruses in your body to assist you avoid diseases. Continuous absence of sleep changes the workings of your immune cells. They may not attack as fast, and often you may get sick.

A Healthy Heart

Your cardiovascular system suffers from inflammation and stress when you deny it the regular sleep pattern it requires. In turn, this can lead to heart conditions and the chance of getting a stroke. Your blood pressure goes down while you sleep, giving a little rest to your heart and blood vessels. The less sleep you get, the longer a 24-hour cycle of your blood pressure stays up. High blood pressure, including stroke, can lead to heart disease.

Better Athletic Performance

If you are into endurance sports like swimming, running, and biking, you might not be doing yourself any favors by denying yourself sufficient sleep. As much as wrestling and weightlifting only require quick bursts of energy, these athletes also require sufficient sleep.

Besides muscle repair time, you are robbing yourself of energy. Your motivation will drain out because its main propeller is sleep. This means you will have a harder time getting to the finish line. No athletes want that.

If for a second you thought that getting enough sleep does not matter that much, think again. For our emotional well-being and physical health, a good night's sleep is essential. That is why you should never underestimate the benefits of a nice sleep. The ability to attain proper rest on a regular basis is not just a good idea; it is an important one.

Chapter 8: The Future of Meditation

The art of mediation has existed for centuries and its influence is only getting stronger. With the aid of technology, people who were once in doubt about the practice are getting into it through guided meditations and apps that simplify things. People can now know when they are doing it right.

The internet has transformed the practice since one does not need to go find a teacher to learn. Instead, they rely on guided tapes and videos to learn the art. In this chapter, a little light is shed on the reach of meditation and the technology present.

The Spread and Reach of Meditation

The practice of meditation is believed to have been going on well before written history. Its roots can be traced back to organized religious frameworks and beliefs in the East. It began its spread to Western culture in the 1960s and since then research on meditation has experienced tremendous growth as interest toward Eastern beliefs and philosophies has also grown. Since then, the rapid spread and expansion of meditation have been influenced by scientists, clinicians, theorists, health practitioners and nonprofessionals who understand the practical benefits of meditation, especially in contemporary culture. These individuals and other meditators advocate for making meditation legitimate as a universal and non-sectarian practice as it unfolds many benefits and positive outcomes for mind, body, and soul, allowing us to experience the essence and fullness of life.

Over the past few years, meditation has achieved widespread popularity as one of the pillars of wellbeing alongside a healthy diet and exercise. Some people have even predicted that meditation will be among the next big public health revolutions. The trend has begun with promising positive results, especially in our current digitally addicted, demanding, and stressful times. The "Mindful Revolution" has taken the media by storm by announcing is the new focus-restoring and anxiety-attacking secret for everyone from government representatives to Silicon Valley entrepreneurs. This heavy globalization has also confused the practice and concept. The mixing of different meditation techniques as well has highly influenced the devaluing of the technique and can, in turn, begin losing its initial spiritual meaning.

Meditation and Technology

Even with the spread of meditation, some people still do not meditate either due to lack of knowledge or due to lack of time. This was an opportunity for technology to come to do what it does best and make it easier for us to practice and manage. It began with the introduction of audio and videotapes for meditation, which made it easier to meditate as one did not have to go in search of a meditation teacher. The rise of the internet also gave a jump-start to the widespread making meditation more accessible to people from all over the world. Apps like

Headspace, Buddhify, and Calm have made meditation easily accessible by allowing users to experience mindfulness with the ease of simply downloading an app and getting started. Apps are also currently developing to wearable technology such as the Moodmetric smart ring, which works with a mobile phone app to keep track of your stress activity, stressors, triggers, and relaxers. These apps also make meditation practice more efficient and convenient as one can do it at whatever point of the day, they feel free, and as it is just a swipe away.

Chapter 9: Techniques to Try Out

With so many techniques already mentioned, learning a couple more might seem 'too much.' However, these are specifically for the end. One of them combines three techniques while the other is the most popular and most scientifically studied. As you carry on with the practice, you will find out that many different ones share the same similarities or stem from one.

It is also okay to try different techniques until you feel that you have found the one that serves your purpose. In this chapter, we look into these meditation techniques and how by studying them, you can be able to get rid of your anxiety.

Vipassana Meditation

Vipassana is one of India's most ancient meditation techniques, which means seeing things as they really are. The idea behind Vipassana is self-observation and self-purification. The foundation of the practice is the observation of breath in an effort to concentrate the mind. You observe the changing nature of body and mind with a sharp awareness and experience the universal truths of impermanence, suffering and being egoless. The meditation of Vipassana seeks the greatest spiritual goals of complete liberation and enlightenment. Its intention is not merely to heal physical disease. However, many psychosomatic illnesses face eradication as a byproduct of mental purification.

Yes, the Buddha brought it about but it is completely non-dogmatic and universal.

All students who decide to take part in the course should fully submit themselves for 10 days to the course and observe what "noble silence." This means that during the 10-day course, you are restricted from making any contact with other meditators; may it be physical, eye contact or speech. Students can speak with the teacher whenever necessary. The noble silence is an important part of the practice.

Attendees also need to follow the following rules:

- No killing of any being
- No stealing of property
- No telling of lies
- No consumption of any toxic substances
- No engaging in any violent activity

The course is completely free and receives motion from donations from people who have finished and seen the benefits of Vipassana meditation. They do not accept your donation of the latter are not observed. Neither the teacher nor volunteers receive any monetary payment. This is so worldwide.

The full course follows strict time guidelines with students waking up at 4 a.m. and beginning their meditation in the hall by 4.30 a.m. Following a tea break, lunch break, and another tea break, in that order during the day, the day ends with a night meditation and a discourse by S.N. Goenka (also the teacher) to explain the events of the day.

Through the practice, people get to learn that many problems in life are avertable by just observing the sensation one experiences through the body. The more one gets to understand how they feel when different sensations occur, the more they can be able to understand their emotions. Through the practice, you experience that even addictions do not stem from the source of addiction but from the body sensations one experiences while indulging in them.

Why 10 days? Well, the course is a systematic process and the introduction of different progressive techniques happens gradually. In order, the techniques taught are mindful breathing, mindful body, and Metta, also known as love and kindness meditation.

Vipassana is a technique designed by Buddha to rid the mind of impurities, to prevent one from reacting blindly when confronted by unpleasant realities and to stop creating tension while remaining in harmony and peace with oneself and others. When you decide to bury negativity within you, you will not have solved the solution. By choosing to vocalize it, you are only creating more problems for oneself and others. The best way to deal with any unpleasant encounter is to observe it and watch it go away. This way you will be free of it.

Through Vipassana, people have been able to eradicate diseases from their bodies. It is the belief of the practice that many diseases occur because of the negativities we bottle up in ourselves. By removing the negativities in you, your diseases may disappear or alleviate. However, it is not advisable to attend the practice with the thought of getting cures in mind. By doing this, you will be focusing on the wrong goal and might not get/ or worsen the results you expect.

Overall, input from previous students testify on the benefits of the technique. Many students end up going for every consecutive sitting after their first because of the mental and physical benefits that occur. Addicts, people suffering from body ailments, anxiety and panic disorders are all body sensations. Maybe this practice is for you.

Transcendental Meditation

This form of meditation is one of the most studied forms of meditation. It is clear, through the help of research to be quite effective at dealing with stress, blood pressure, and anxiety. The practice carries many more benefits though. Its popularity gained the attention of the Beatles among other celebrities. Just like any meditation practice, the more you practice the more the benefits reveal themselves.

Transcendental meditation differs from mindful meditation in a number of ways. With mindful meditation, when your thoughts drift off, you are required to refocus your attention on the present moment. With transcendental, you are required to repeat a simple mantra while paying attention to the sensations that keep coming and going. Under the guidance of an instructor, learning the technique takes four days but can be somewhat costly.

During a 60-minute introductory lesson, a TM teacher provides general data on the method and its impacts. This accompanies the second lesson of 45 minutes giving information that is more specific. People interested in studying the method will then attend an interview of 10-15 minutes and 1-2 hours of private training. Everyone receives a secret mantra after a brief ceremony. Later on, the teacher is responsible for providing details on the benefits of its practice, explains details about the practice and make any corrections that may be necessary.

Numerous studies back up the success of the meditation technique. It has shown to be effective in stress reduction, anxiety management, mental, and physical health. In addition, it is helpful in dealing with insomnia, depression, autism, addictions and even PTSD. People practice transcendental meditation between fifteen to twenty minutes twice a day. Some people report that meditation worsens the symptoms of some psychiatric conditions. It is advisable to consult a professional medical practitioner before indulging in meditation.

These meditation techniques have different components in them that make them interesting. It is for the interest of the readers only that this is present in the book. I concur; so many meditation techniques are available. You are free to choose the one that resonates best with you.

Your most important companion is your mind. Your mind is directly responsible for the quality of life you live. You are the cause of your joy and sadness. The more you meditate, the more some of these facts become clear and present themselves. As you progress with the practice, certain truths such as the love for oneself begin to show themselves as well. Most people believe that the source of their joy and sadness lies with someone else. This is very untrue.

As one continues to dive deeper into the practice, one begins to notice increased levels of self-respect and self-love. It is by cultivating the virtues we have in ourselves that we can help others cultivate theirs. The above two meditation techniques (as well as the rest) can start one off to an amazing journey of self-discovery. The practice is bound to be of benefit to both the present and the future practitioners of this art. Meditation is universal. Use it wisely.

Conclusion

Thank you for making it all the way to the end of this book. If you have gotten to this point it is because you are committed to learning about the ways in which meditation can have a profoundly positive effect in your life.

As such, the next step is to put what you have learned into practice. That is, from the reduction of stress, anxiety, insomnia and even pain, the benefits of meditations somewhat keep mocking its naysayers. The more research conducted, the more the previous sentence makes sense. Thousands of research reports continue to prove how meditation influences both the mental and physical wellbeing. Meditation can bridge the gap between you and many worldly wants as well: your sleep gets better, you are able to regulate your weight, your relationships become more satisfactory and you have the ability to reduce physical pains that occasionally come and go.

Although its practice is still being blindsided by many factors, the practice is bound to receive the recognition it deserves eventually. With the internet of things, the spread of the practice is almost reaching a rampant state with the topic of meditation resting on the lips of both professionals and paupers. Even in the event that most of these people are just talking about it without putting any practice, the fact that it has gained such a massive amount of popularity is nothing but astounding. This is a positive thing though, as the positives of meditation outweigh the negatives.

For those who are a bit skeptical about engaging in it because of various reasons, I hope this book serves as a beacon of light to dispel any misbeliefs and doubts one might carry about the practice. The main purpose of meditation is to reach within and access oneself. We all spend so much time on a daily basis trying to find people and things. It all falls in place easier if you discover the most important thing to find is yourself.

So, thank you once again for your kind attention. If you have found this book to be useful or helpful, in any way, please tell your friends and family, or anyone whom you believe to be interested in this topic, about this book. It will surely help them find the balance they seek in life. In addition, they are surely going to benefit in the long run.

Thanks again and see you in the next one!

CPSIA information can be obtained
at www.ICGtesting.com
Printed in the USA
LVHW020459120221
679113LV00015B/483